LANDMARK

C000041152

Ticino

Andrew Beattie & Tim Pepper

Andrew Beattie read geography at Mansfield College, Oxford, and teaches the subject at Eltham College, London. He has accompanied groups of pupils to destinations as diverse as Bavaria and the Dead Sea, and has travelled widely in Europe, the Middle East and India. He is the author of a number of travel articles, and of three published plays.

Tim Pepper read history at Wadham College, Oxford, and has been writing and travelling ever since. He has written for the *Independent on Sunday* and the *International Dictionary of Historic Places,* and his travels have taken him from the deserts of Jordan and Syria to the jungles of Mexico. He lives in Buckinghamshire.

Andrew Beattie and Tim Pepper are the authors of *The Visitor's Guide to Hungary, Off the Beaten Track: the Czech and Slovak Republics, Landmark Visitor's Guide: Cracow* (in this series) and *The Rough Guide to Syria.*

Acknowledgements

Thanks to Juliusz Komarnicki, long-time Lugano resident, for his advice about the manuscript; Eugenio Foglia at Ticino Turismo in Bellinzona; and to Lyn, whose legs are just about now recovering from our assault on the Passo di Gana Negra.

TICINO

ZURICH / LUCERNE

DISENTIS

St Gotthard Pass/
Passo del San Gottardo

Gotthard
Tunnel

Lukmanier Pass/
Passo del Lucomagno

①

Olivone

CHUR

Airolo

Nufenenpass/
Passo della Novena

②

San
Bernardino
Tunnel

③

BRIG
GENEVA

Fusio

⑤

San Bernardino

San Carlo

Rossa

Bosco
Gurin

Sonogno

Biasca

Bignasco

Cevio

Grono

Locarno

Bellinzona

Camedo

DOMODOSSOLA

④

⑥

ITALY

Lake Maggiore

Lugano

Lake Lugano

Menaggio

Lúino

Lake Como

Laveno

Porto
Cerésio

Mendrisio

Chiasso

N

Varese

Como

W   E

MILAN

MILAN

S

| 0 | 5 | 10 miles |

| 0 | 5 | 10km |

Opposite: Lavertezzo

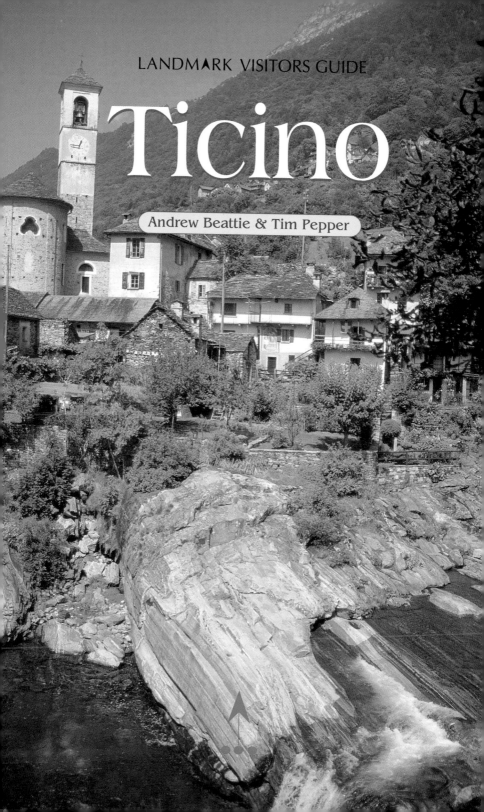

LANDMARK VISITORS GUIDE

Ticino

Andrew Beattie & Tim Pepper

• CONTENTS •

*I*ntroduction

The Ticino forms a triangle of land which juts south from central Switzerland into Italy. Almost exclusively Italian speaking, it's rather cut off from the rest of the country, with many of its linguistic, cultural and historical ties focussed towards Milan rather than Zurich (the two cities which lie closest to it). It's a favourite holiday destination for German speakers (from both Germany and northern Switzerland), but receives comparatively fewer English-speaking visitors. Its attractions are twofold, and are the attraction of Switzerland as a whole: namely, lakes and mountains.

In the southern Ticino, Lake Maggiore and Lake Lugano straddle the border with Italy; the principal resorts on both lakes, respectively the cities of Locarno and Lugano, both lie in Swiss territory, and are the major focus for visitors. Lugano, the canton's largest city, has an international airport, rail connections with Germany and Italy, and an internationally-oriented residential community. Both cities have a varied and extensive cultural life, with the Locarno Film Festival one of the most respected international film events of the year.

Surrounding the lakes, and stretching north to a height of over 10,000ft (3,000m), are the Alps, providing wonderful opportunities for walking in the summer, and (less importantly) skiing in the winter. Outdoor tourism forms a major part of the region's economy: besides walking and skiing there is plenty of opportunity for watersports, golf, cycling, fishing, or just getting in a cable car and ascending a precipitous mountainside to enjoy the view. The region also has a rich architectural heritage, with a fine Romanesque architectural tradition dating from the time when it was essentially part of northern Italy.

All in all the Ticino offers travellers a myriad of things to do and see in a comparatively small area: it only takes two hours to travel by train from one end of the canton to the other (Chiasso in the south, on the Italian border, to Airolo in the north, at the foot of the St Gotthard Pass), making it possible to actually see the whole area from one base, and to get to know it well in a fairly short space of time.

History

The history of Switzerland as a nation state really dates back to 1291, when the cantons of Schwyz, Uri and Unterwalden (forming the area around Lucerne to the north of the St Gotthard Pass) declared a 'perpetual alliance' against the dynastic and imperialist policies of the Habsburgs. In 1315 these intentions were sealed in victory on the battlefield, when the cantons beat the Habsburgs at Morgarten.

Throughout the course of the fourteenth century, the Swiss Confederacy expanded, first towards the east (taking territory from the Austrians) and then towards the north and west. In the early fifteenth century, the largely French-speaking canton of Valais broke away from Savoy to join the Confederacy, and about this time the Confederation actively began to seek influence in the Ticino, largely to ensure control of the south, as well as the north, approach to the Gotthard.

The Ticino essentially consists of the territory captured by the Swiss Confederacy from the duchy of Milan between 1440 and 1516; the most decisive battle fought during this time was at Giornico, just north of Biasca on the Ticino river, in 1478.

During the Thirty Years War (1618-1648) the Confederacy remained neutral, and Switzerland, including the districts of Bellinzona and Lugano, was recognised as an independent nation state for the first time by the Treaty of Westphalia, which concluded the war. After the occupation of Switzerland by France from 1798 to 1803 these districts became Canton Ticino and were declared a full part of Switzerland under Napoleon's Mediation Acts of 1803; in 1815 the Peace of Paris recognised the boundaries of Switzerland in their present-day form. Bellinzona, Locarno and Lugano took it in turns to be capital of the canton until 1878 when Bellinzona became the region's permanent political capital.

In 1991 the seven hundredth anniversary celebrations of the founding of the Confederation opened in the Courtyard of the Castelgrande in Bellinzona (although the country's true historical heart lies in Schwyz, near Lake Lucerne, where the original Perpetual Alliance was signed).

Upper and Lower Ticino

The major division among the inhabitants of the Ticino is whether or not you come from the Sopra Ceneri (the mountain area, including Locarno) or the Sottoceneri (the lowlands around Lugano and Chiasso). The dividing line is the the Monte Ceneri pass between Bellinzona and Lugano. The Sottocenreri people consider themselves a cut above the mountain dwellers and hill farmers of the Sopraceneri.

Modern Switzerland

Switzerland is full of contradictions as a nation state: it is a highly advanced society, with an economy based on tourism, banking, service industries, precision engineering, and heavier industries such as chemicals; its people enjoy one of the highest standards of living in the world; it is a country of stable government which hasn't fought a war against a foreign power for two hundred years; it lies at the centre of Europe, with foreigners forming a large proportion of its residents and with a lot of European trade and road and rail traffic passing through it; its cities are thoroughly modern, world centres, with Geneva the home to many international organisations and Zurich one of the world's great banking capitals.

Yet, it steadfastly refuses to join the European Union or the United Nations (membership of both organisations was rejected in referenda in 1992 and 1986). Women did not gain full voting rights in some parts of the country until as recently as 1991, and it is one of the most tightly controlled countries in the western world, where rules, state interference and police powers have a much greater influence in the running of things than they do in any other country in Europe.

Economy

The main centres of Swiss industry are rather distant from the Ticino: the chemical, precision technology, pharmaceuticals, watch and metal industries are all located in the north of the country, in cities such as Basel, Zurich and St Gallen, and industries in the Ticino are predominantly light engineering and food processing firms.

The economy of the canton is based on these activities, plus agriculture and tourism; Lugano has also emerged as an important banking centre, and many valleys in the mountainous north of the canton have been dammed for the generation of hydroelectricity, some of which is exported to Italy. It is a wealthy canton, strengthened particularly as a result of the influx of retired people from Germany who come to live out their days in the balmy climate of the lakes.

Government

Switzerland is a thoroughly decentralised state where local government often assumes a far greater relevance to people than the national, federal government. Ticino is one of the twenty-six Swiss cantons, which gradually grew up from an original alliance of three cantons in 1291, centred on Canton Schwyz near Lake Lucerne, which gave its name to the whole country.

The Ticino has been a canton with its own government since 1803. It is divided into smaller units, communes, which are independent bodies, fixing their own budgets and raising taxes. Like all other cantons Ticino has its own parliament, legislature and judiciary, and it sends two representatives to sit on the Council of States which forms one part of the government of the Confederation of Switzerland.

Legislation is famously often fixed by referenda, which have included a national vote to legally establish the equality of men and women (1980), the introduction of motorway tolls (1985), and the construction of a new, fast rail
(cont'd on page 12)

• WALKING •

In Ticino the skiing may be disappointing, but the hiking definitely isn't! The area is a walker's paradise, with magnificent views across peaks, valleys and lakes, particularly in the north, around Airolo, and Robiei, north of Locarno. Walks of varying difficulties are mentioned in each chapter.

Direction signposts point walkers the right way at path junctions, or outside cable car or railway stations. In the mountains most paths are marked by red and white markers painted onto rocks and walls at intervals (low altitude paths are usually marked with yellow markers, and the highest paths by white and blue markers).

Walkers should ensure that they are properly equipped with rainwear, proper boots, and food and drink; walking on a hot days leads to thirst very quickly, but don't peel off too many layers or the sometimes sun will burn you.

A map is absolutely essential (see FactFile), as sometimes trails are slightly vague. You can assume that paths above 5,000ft (1,500m) will be rocky, and steep and difficult in places. Most paths are open

Right:
Il Sosto,
Blenio

Opposite page: Hiking between San Carlo & Robiei, Val Bavona

between May and September/October, depending on how high they go. A network of mountain huts run by the Swiss and Ticinese Alpine Associations provides walkers with dormitory accommodation, meals and shelter in the mountains (see FactFile and individual entries in each chapter).

The international Alpine distress signal is a series of six signals given at regular intervals within a minute by whatever means are available (whistle blasts, shouts, torch flashes), followed by a minute's pause, followed by a repetition of the signals. The 'answer', acknowledging the distress signal, is three signals at regular intervals within a minute.

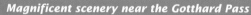

Magnificent scenery near the Gotthard Pass

route over the Alps at a cost of up to $2,000m (1991). In November 1989 a referendum to abolish the army was defeated, although a third of the voters were in favour of abolition, and in 1994 the Swiss people voted that the national army should not take part in United Nations Peace Keeping activities in the world's trouble spots.

Switzerland & the UN

Switzerland is not a member of the European Union or of the United Nations, but it *is* a member of various subsidiary UN bodies, including the World Health Organisation, UNICEF, UNESCO and the Food and Agriculture Organisation. In addition it is a member of the European Free Trade Association and the Council of Europe, and since 1977 it has had a free trade agreement with the European Union.

It is completely surrounded by EU states (France, Germany, Austria and Italy) and a fair amount of EU trade passes through the country (a lot of it via the Gotthard and through the Ticino).

Military service

Although the country has not been involved in a war since 1803, it maintains a big standing army: all males between twenty and fifty years old serve in the military, with regular 'refresher' courses after the initial period of military training, and with no provision for performing civilian duties (such as community service) instead of military service. Details of military service can be seen pinned up outside town halls, community buildings in villages, and at railway stations, under the heading *Tiro Obligatoro* ('Compulsory Service'). Men keep their weapons at home at all times.

Most bridges and other structures are built so that they can be blown up easily to thwart the progress of an advancing foreign army through the mountains, and all houses are provided with shelters against fallout from a nuclear war.

Swiss peculiarities

The country is highly regulated, with strange rules against all sorts of things (such as legal times when cars can be washed) which would be unthinkable in other countries. The police are alleged to keep extensive files on the activities of a comparatively large number of Swiss citizens, and the country has been accused of holding many people in prison without trial, leading some to suggest that the country is run in some ways like a police state.

Despite (or because of) this, the Swiss are an excessively law-abiding people, who go to bed early, commit comparatively few crimes, tend to be formal and polite in introductions and conversations, and who seem content to enjoy their massively prosperous lifestyle whilst only taking as much notice of the world outside their own country as they deem necessary.

Eating

The food of the region is predictably Italian based but lacks the character of authentic Italian cuisine, being more in line with the fast-food interpretation found in

12

most western European towns and cities – certainly as regards the pizza and pasta dishes.

Some authentic Lombard influences do permeate the border though; appetisers (antipasto) consist of various cold meats and vegetable dishes – prosciutto (ham, either cooked or cured) and salame (salami) are the most common choices. Popular mainstays of the main courses are polenta, yellow cornmeal, boiled and served hot with butter and cheese or as an accompaniment to a meat dish, and risotto (Lombardy being a major rice producer).

Predictably, a wide variety of fish is available, especially trout, pike, perch, tench and eel, as are a range of traditional beef and poultry dishes. Ethnic restaurants have not really entered the region, though sadly the burger bars have.

Drinking

The Merlot wines that the Ticino is justly renowned for only arrived in the region from Bordeaux in 1905 after the entire vineyards of the canton were decimated by the phylloxera plague. Today nearly 85 per cent of the Ticino vineyards are devoted to Merlot and they produce around 90,000 gallons (4 million litres) of delicately perfumed wine every year.

Merlot is essentially a red wine but you can also find rosé and white versions which are produced by removing the skin from the fermenting juice. The largest vineyards are in the southern Ticino, particularly in the villages of Castel San Pietro and Stabio.

The region produces two spirits; grappa and nocino. Grappa is a

Wine-tasting in the Ticino

Several cellars are open to the public for wine-tasting and buying. The following is a selection where English is spoken. In all cases phone first for an appointment.

Fratelli Matasci
6598 Tenero
☎ (091) 735 60 11

Vini Delea
Via Zandone 11, 6616 Losone
☎ (091) 791 08 17

Cantina Monti
Ai Ronchi, 6936 Cademario
☎ (091) 605 34 75

Cantine Badaracco
Via Pedemonte, 6816 Melano
☎ (091) 649 93 35

Cantina Sociale Mendrisio
Via Bernasconi 22, 6850 Mendrisio
☎ (091) 646 46 21

I vini di Guido Brivio SA
Via Vignoo 8, 6850 Mendrisio
☎ (091) 646 07 57

brandy produced from the refuse of pressed grapes – there are over 10,000 producers of the stuff in the region, many of them family distilleries, though the production quality is always closely monitored by the state.

Nocino is a nut liquor also known by the colloquial name Ratafià (meaning literally 'it's done'). It's a liquid produced in mysterious circumstances by only a couple of companies, a handful of families and the monks of Bigorio and is delicious on top of vanilla ice-cream!

Italian – some useful phrases

English	Italian	Pronunciation
Yes/no	Sì/no	See/no
That's fine	Va bene	Va baynay
Good morning	Buon giorno	Bwon jorno
Good evening	Buona sera	Bwona saira
Good night	Buona notte	Bwona nottay
Goodbye	Arrivederci	Arreevedairchee
Hi/bye	Ciao	Chow
My name is...	Mi chiamo...	Mee kyama
(No) Thank you	(No) Grazie	(No) Gratzeeay
Yes please	Sì grazie	See gratzeeay
Please (offering)	Prego	Praygo
Please (asking)	Per favore	Pair favoray
Sorry	Scusi	Skoozee
How much is it?	Quanto costa?	Kwanto kosta
Where is the...?	Dov'è il/la...?	Doveh eel/la
Cheers	Alla salute	Alla salootay
I don't understand	Non capisco	Non kapeesko
Do you speak English?	Parla inglese	Parla eenglayzay
Help	Aiuto	I-ooto
Sunday	Domenica	Domeneeka
Monday	Lunedì	Oonedee
Tuesday	Martedì	Artedee
Wednesday	Mercoledì	Mairkoledee
Thursday	Giovedì	Govedee
Friday	Venerdì	Venairdee
Saturday	Sabato	Sabato
Today	Oggi	Ojee
Yesterday	Ieri	Airee
Tomorrow	Domani	Domanee
Minute	Minuto	Menooto
Hour	Ora	Ora
Day	Giorno	Jorno
Week	Settimana	Setteemana
Month	Mese	Mayzay
Year	Anno	Anno
0	Zero	Tzairo
1	Uno	Oono
2	Due	Dooay
3	Tre	Tray
4	Quattro	Kwattro
5	Cinque	Cheenkway
6	Sei	Say
7	Sette	Settay
8	Otto	Otto
9	Nove	Novay
10	Dieci	Deeaychee

Birra (beer) is readily available in the region, the ever-present brand is Cardinal Lager who seem to have sewn up most of the local market. It's not bad but do be wary of the practice in some of these parts of watering it down with sugar water (entirely legal), ultimately turning it into a panaché (shandy).

The usual range of soft drinks and acqua minerale (mineral waters) are of course available, as is tea and coffee. Coffee, unless otherwise stated, will be the strong, black variety espresso. Alternatives you can ask for are caffe macchiato, which is basically espresso with a bit of milk, cappuccino, a milky, frothy coffee sprinkled with cocoa, and caffelatte (white coffee).

Language

Italian is the language of the Ticino, though German, and to a lesser extent French, are widely understood. This is, however, slightly off the beaten track for

Left: Corippo in the Verzasca valley

Below: Isole di Brissago, a unique botanical garden

Bottom: Ascona

most English tourists and so English is not as readily understood as you might expect outside of the main resorts of Como, Lugano and Locarno.

The Ticino is very much a passage way from northern and central Europe to Italy, many travellers pausing to break journeys here before moving on. A smattering of Italian will go a long way for you at hotels and restaurants. A box on the page 14 displays some of the more useful phrases.

Geology

The Alps form the principal point of interest to most visitors to Switzerland; one-seventh of the total area of these mountains lies in Switzerland, and they occupy around sixty per cent of the country's land area. Virtually all of the Ticino is mountainous, from the first stirrings of the Alps in the south, to the highest peak, Campo Tencia, whose summit reaches 10,078ft (3,072m).

The Gotthard massif, which forms the northern border of Ticino, is the source of the rivers Rhein, Rhone and Ticino, and is the geographical centre of the Swiss Alps. The mountains are spectacular, particularly in the northern part of the canton around Airolo, but do not reach the 13,000ft (4,000m) plus altitude of the western Alps on the Franco-Swiss border.

The Alps are young, active fold mountains, formed in the past one hundred million years by the collision of the Eurasian and African tectonic plates, which caused the surface of the earth to buckle and fold upwards to produce the spectacular mountains we see today. The mountains were cut down by rivers, and by glaciers – mighty rivers of ice, which cut broad, steep-sided U-shaped valleys such as the Valle Leventina between Bellinzona and Airolo – which flowed south, depositing a huge amount of eroded material in what was once the western arm of the Adriatic and which is now the flat plain of northern Italy.

Most of the rocks forming the Alps are marine (sea-floor) sediments or alluvial (river) deposits; fossilised remains of sea creatures can still be found in many parts of the mountains. Monte San Salvatore, near Lugano, is formed from dolomite limestone, a marine sedimentary rock built up beneath the sea.

The area is still an active zone of mountain building by tectonic forces, and of down-cutting by the erosive forces of rivers. During colder periods of ice advance in the past, huge glaciers moved south from the high mountains to gouge out the valleys of the southern Ticino, which later on became filled with water, forming the characteristically long, thin, finger-like lakes of Lugano, Maggiore and Como. These lakes are much longer than they are wide, and they are also very deep: the bottom of Lake Maggiore, in particular, is well below sea level.

Flora

The Ticino has a mild, wet climate, with vegetation ranging from sub-tropical palm trees by Lake Maggiore to Alpine meadowlands on the mountains. Many plants are protected by federal law, and picking them is illegal. On the lower slopes of the mountains are pine, beech and chestnut forests; the latter derive from the sweet chestnut trees introduced to the area by the Romans, and are widely seen in the Ticino.

Chestnuts

Chestnuts once formed the major part of the diet of mountain dwellers in the Ticino; they could be ground down to make flour for bread. Now many chestnut trees are threatened by a fungus of American origin. Chestnut trees can be identified through their serrated, elongated leaves, as opposed to the dark green oval leaves of beech trees.

At higher altitudes, beech and chestnut forests give way to spruce, larch and pine trees and then to Alpine pastures and heathland which finally becomes bare rock. Alpine rhododendrons, characterised by dark red leaves, are the most common heathland plants. The permanent snowline is at 9,100ft (2,800m), and only a few mountains in the Ticino are snow covered all year round.

Wildlife

Up in the mountains, above an altitude of 4,300ft (1,300m), walkers will come across small, brown, shy and rather cute creatures called Alpine marmots. They live in colonies of around fifty creatures, and build extensive systems of burrows, down which they usually dart at the first signs of people.

They pass much of their time in the summer sitting on rocks emitting high-pitched shrieks, which are intended as warning signs for the other members of their communities, and which echo eerily around the usually silent valleys. During the winter they hibernate in their burrows, the entrances to which are blocked up with rocks and grass.

Other forms of mountain wildlife include golden eagles, which have a wing span of up to 8ft (2.5m) and which feed extensively on marmots (particularly the slow ones) and hares, which are largely nocturnal and feed on plants in the heathland zone. Lower down in woodland areas roe deer, foxes and lizards, which like sunning themselves on rocks and zooming into crevices at the first sign of approaching life, can be seen.

North-Western Ticino:
the Gotthard and the Valle Leventina

NORTH-WESTERN TICINO

Map key and labels:

KEY
- ---- Cable Car
- .... Walks
- .... Glacier

LUCERNE / ZURICH · Göschenen
Andermatt
CANTON URI
St Gotthard Road & Rail Tunnels
Ravetsch
Capanna Cadlimo · VAL CADLIMO
DISENTIS
Lukmanier Pass (Passo del Lucomagno)
Realp
Furka
Gletsch
Furka Pass
Capanna Cadagno
St Gothard Pass (Passo del San Gottardo)
CANTON VALAIS
Oberwald
Airolo
Lago Ritòm
Passo dell' Uomo
Olivone
Furka Rail Tunnel · Rotondo
Ulrichen
Piora Funicular rly
Nufenenpass (Passo della Novena)
Bedretto Ronco
Pescium
Quinto
Carì
BIASCA
BRIG / GENEVA
Piotta
Ambri
VALLE LEVENTINA
Faido
Griessee
All'Acqua
Lago del Naret
Rodi
Dalpe
Piana Selva
Griesgletscher
Robiei · Capanna Basodino
Fusio
Campo Tencia
River Ticino
ITALY
San Carlo
Giornico
0 — 6 miles
0 — 6km
LOCARNO
BIASCA / BELLINZONA / LUGANO

The region of the north-western Ticino is, for many travellers, their introduction to Italian Switzerland. Those entering the canton by road and rail after a journey through Europe from the UK, or after getting in a train or hire car at Zurich Airport, will pass through the Gotthard tunnels and emerge into the southern Alps at Airolo, the largest town and most important transport focus of this region.

Airolo is not particularly interesting in itself, but nowhere in this chapter is more than fifty minutes from the town by road or rail, making it the most obvious centre for visiting this region; and with distances so short, coming here from Biasca (Chapter Two), Bellinzona (Chapter Three) or even from the lakes is very easy.

The Alps to the south of Airolo reach more than 9,850ft (3,000m) – the highest in the Ticino – so it is not surprising that most visitors here are skiers and walkers, or at least are on the lookout for fine scenery. The biggest skiing centre is **Airolo** itself, which is covered, with the St Gotthard Pass, in the first part of this chapter.

Running west from Airolo is the picturesque **Val Bedretto** which runs up to another pass, the **Nufenenpass** (Passo della Novena), with a number of opportunities for walking. East from Airolo, railway and motorway run along the **Valle Leventina** towards Bellinzona, the lakes and Italy; there are some scenic diversions along the valley, described in the last part of the chapter, following a detailed description of the walks and scenery around **Lago Ritóm** which lies a short distance to the east of Airolo and which is the most popular focus for summer visitors in the area.

Travelling the St Gotthard Pass (Passo del San Gottardo)

The St Gotthard motorway and rail tunnels link Airolo in the Ticino with Göschenen in the Reuss valley to the north in Canton Uri, a distance of around 10 miles (15km). The Gotthard tunnels form one of the most important routeways through the Alps for both road and rail traffic. The road tunnel is on the Milan-Lucerne (Milano-Luzern) motorway, giving access from north-western Italy to northern Switzerland, Zurich and Germany. Most trains operating through the tunnel link the Ticino with central and northern Switzerland, running from Chiasso via Lugano, Bellinzona and Biasca through the tunnel to Zurich and Basel. International trains operate from Milan, and cities further south into Italy, through the tunnel into Germany and even as far as Amsterdam and Brussels.

The tunnels are operational all year, but the road pass over the mountains, which has been rendered irrelevant by the major trunk route via the tunnels, is not cleared of snow and so is open only from May to October.

The road pass runs from Airolo up to the hotel, restaurant and museum complex at the summit of the pass (by the old *ozpizio* or hospice, situated at 6,860ft/2,091m) before dropping down to the mountain resort of Andermatt (4,710ft/1,436m) and then reaching Göschenen a short distance north of here, where drivers can re-join the motorway to Lucerne if desired. Driving from Airolo to Göschenen takes under an hour. During summer there are three buses a day in each direction over the pass, linking Airolo and Andermatt in around fifty minutes, and calling at the restaurant/museum at the pass summit.

AIROLO AND THE
PASSO DEL SAN GOTTARDO

Airolo itself is rather a shabby place. Once it was a major coaching and trading post, the last stop on the road up to the Gotthard: this is where the road started getting steep. But now traffic heading up the pass takes a route which avoids the centre of Airolo, negotiating interchanges and criss-crossing the valley by means of an ugly set of concrete-piered flyovers which, on a map, look like uncoiled spaghetti.

At around 5pm every afternoon in summer, the town has a reminder of its former role, when tourists sweep elegantly along the main street in an open-top carriage, riding in a mock-up of the nineteenth century postbuses which once headed up to the pass from here. The arrival of this horse-drawn contraption from Andermatt, on the other side of the pass, is heralded by blasts on the driver's hand-held horn and the ringing of church bells in Airolo. It's the only thing to wake Airolo from its slumbers, apart from the occasional revving of motorcycles by their drivers who have forgotten the presence of a bypass.

The town is built around a street which runs uphill from the station, past the tourist office and post office, before it turns a hairpin bend and takes a narrow course between cafés and hotels with shuttered upper floors. Airolo is the best walking and skiing base in the upper Ticino and has a range of hotels: the best are opposite the station, the cheaper ones are up the road and round the corner.

In the west of the town, the motorway and the railway make a right-hand turn and disappear – without any fuss – into the valley side. The entrances to the 15-mile (24km) long Gotthard road and rail tunnels are unremarkable and unmarked by any road or trackside announcements. Outside the station is a memorial to those who died building the Gotthard rail tunnel.

In Airolo

There are two specific things to head for in Airolo. The most obvious is the **cable car**, whose lower station is on the town's southern edge next to the motorway junction (a walk of twenty minutes from the railway station). It runs up to **Pesciüm** with a second stage to **Sasso della Boggia**. At Pesciüm there are ski tows and a restaurant the size of a small aircraft hangar, heaving with gently steaming skiers in winter and usually practically empty in summer.

A number of walks start from here, including the Strada degli Alpi, an easy walk running along the valley side, eastwards from Pesciüm to Lago Tremorgio, and westwards to villages in the Val Bedretto. More ambitious hikes head over the Sassello or Sassi passes into the Cristallina range and the area described in the walking box on pages 90-91.

On the road up to the pass is the **Hospice Fort Museum** (*Museo*

(cont'd on page 25)

THE GOTTHARD
– a way through the mountains

There has been a recognised way across the Alps between the Ticino and Reuss valleys since time immemorial; certainly the Romans knew about the Gotthard route, as Roman artefacts have been found in the vicinity of the pass. But little specific history is known about the pass before medieval times, largely due to the loss of documents relating to the pass during French military occupation in 1798 and a series of fires in the Airolo archives.

Among the bare facts which have emerged relating to the history of the pass are that around 1170 St Galdino, Archbishop of Milan, consecrated a church at the summit of the pass and dedicated it to St Gotthard, a recently canonised former Bishop of Hildesheim in Germany. Written records indicate that a hospice – a charitable foundation which provided food and shelter for passing travellers – was in operation in 1237.

The road up the Gotthard Pass

Over the Gotthard Pass by horse and carriage

How long a hospice had been located on the pass is debatable: a seventeenth century historian maintained, with no evidence, that the first hospice was founded on the pass in 620AD. The hospice was in the care of the Archbishop of Milan during the Middle Ages, but by the eighteenth century it had passed into the hands of the Commune of Airolo and had no religious function.

The hospice was looked after by a hospitaller, a lay person, and run as a charity: taxes were levied on passing goods, and travellers who could afford to had to pay their own board and lodging. The hospitaller also farmed land in the surrounding area and made money selling cheese to passing travellers. Poor travellers were sheltered and fed for free, and buried at the charity's expense if they died on the pass (in the so-called 'Chapel of the Dead', a short distance from the summit of the pass).

By 1745 the government of Canton Uri (the German-speaking canton whose territory covered the northern approach to the pass) began campaigning for a new hospice building, complaining in a letter to a cardinal that *"frequently in winter more than one*

(cont'd overleaf)

THE GOTTHARD
– a way through the mountains

(cont'd from previous page)

hundred persons of either sex are lodged in only two rooms, in order that they may benefit from the warmth of the stove. God knows what unseemly things might happen, but it is to be feared that a not inconsiderable number of sins are committed..."

Perhaps as a reaction to all such suspected immorality a Capuchin friary was established at the summit of the pass in 1683. There were never more than two friars there at any one time, but they ministered to travellers and even founded a small boarding school for boys from the Leventina area. The Old Hospice, adjoining the chapel, was built for the friary in 1775 and can still be seen today (the original one was destroyed by an avalanche); the friary closed in 1841 and the building is now used for storage.

Meanwhile the original charitable hospice, owned by the Commune of Airolo, was destroyed in the winter of 1798-9 when a French garrison spent the winter there during one of Napoleon's campaigns (they managed to completely destroy the town of Airolo too).

The Gotthard Hotel was built on this site in 1837, six years after the first road was built over the pass. By 1842 there was a daily mail-coach journey over the pass on a ten-seater mail coach; today, tourists can still travel by an ornate coach over the pass in a style similar to that experienced by nineteenth century travellers.

In 1892 the opening of the rail tunnel sounded the death-knell for the mail coaches, and the importance of the road pass diminished overnight; there has been no winter shelter available on the pass since 1947, and now only between mid-May and mid-October is access to the summit and hotel accommodation available.

In 1972 the whole site was acquired by the Pro-St Gotthard foundation on behalf of the Swiss Nation; in 1982 the chapel was restored and in 1986 the organisation opened the National St Gotthard Museum in the renovated Old Haltings Place (formerly the Gotthard Hotel, whose name is now carried by the former Monte Prossa hotel, opposite the museum).

Forte Ospizio San Gottardo), which is dedicated to the arms, equipment and uniforms worn by soldiers in their defence of the pass from this site between 1894 and 1947.

The Pass

An odd collection of buildings occupy the narrow shelf of land by the small lake at the top of the pass, just twenty minutes by road from Airolo. There's a military presence here, with army stores and a barracks, but there's a big tourist presence too: the **Gotthard Hotel** was originally opened in 1866, while the grey building behind it is the old Capuchin travellers' hospice.

Attached to the hospice is the **chapel**, whose exterior looks nothing like a chapel at all (unless you notice the bell tower, which is more or less hidden by the upper wall of the hospice). In 1975 remains were found under the present building of two former chapels, one of which is believed to have been consecrated in around 1170.

The interior is stark and bare, perhaps matching the landscape in which it is situated. The hexagonal altar is made from three blocks of granite reclaimed from the digging of the motorway tunnel, and above it is a painting of St Gotthard and St Anthony of Padua (1687). The octagonal building behind the chapel and former Capuchin hospice is a stables, now used as a cellar for the storage of cheese made in the surrounding area.

The **National Museum of St Gotthard** is housed in a swish building built on the site of the former Gotthard Hotel which before that was occupied by the charitable hospice owned by the Commune of Airolo. It's a good museum covering the history of the pass from early medieval times to its eclipse by the building of the tunnels which pass under it deep inside the mountain. On the hour, every hour, there's an audio-visual presentation on the history of the pass, with English subtitles, in the upstairs room of the museum.

WEST OF AIROLO – THE VAL BEDRETTO

The Val Bedretto, running west from Airolo and following the course of the river Ticino to its source around the **Nufenenpass**, is a beautiful valley which is often overlooked by travellers eager to press on from Airolo.

The pass, one of the highest in Switzerland, is a minor one, leading into the upper part of Canton Valais, giving direct access to French-speaking parts of Switzerland from the upper Ticino. There's a year-round postbus

service as far as All'Acqua. In summer there are two bus services in each direction across the pass, linking Airolo with Oberwald in upper Valais. There's nothing really specific to aim for, but the villages through which the road passes are pretty, with good examples of upper Ticino architecture, and the summit of the pass gives access to some high-altitude walks.

(cont'd on page 28)

Passo della Tremola, San Gottardo

Laghetto di Piora, Valle Leventina

Opposite: The summit of Nufenenpass, which links the Ticino and Valais cantons

Above: The northerly approach to the Nufenenpass from Canton Valais

Right: The village of Ronco, in the Val Bedretto

Airolo to Nufenenpass summit

It takes around forty minutes to travel by road from Airolo to the summit of the pass, through a sparsely-populated landscape of coniferous woodland and upland Alpine pasture. The road passes directly through the first two villages, **Fontana** and **Ossasco**, with subsequent villages of **Villa** and then **Bedretto** and lastly **Ronco** reachable on a very narrow minor road which runs along the valley sides, on a narrow shelf above the main road up to the pass.

Buses take the route through the villages, of which Bedretto is probably the most attractive, with its wooden houses which are typical of the Gotthard region. Ronco is the last place in the valley which is inhabited year-round; beyond it is **All'Acqua**, the terminus of the bus when the pass is snowed up, and not really much more than a bus turning-circle surrounded by farm buildings.

The whole of this valley is notorious for winter avalanches, and the villages are protected by a series of concrete defence measures which are positioned on the mountainsides above them to deflect snow slides.

Beyond All'Acqua the road ascends the pass in a series of hairpin bends, overshadowed by the high peaks of the Cristallina range to the south; snow remains on the ground in numerous sheltered pockets around here right through the year.

The Nufenenpass (Passo della Novena)

The road across this pass was opened in 1969 – comparatively late – and the restaurant at the top, set in bleak scenery with excellent views of the Upper Valaisian Alps, was opened shortly afterwards. The pass marks the boundary between German and Italian speaking Switzerland, and between cantons Ticino and Valais (Wallis to German speakers) whose flags fly at the top of the pass. The pass also marks an important watershed, with precipitation falling on the east side flowing into the Ticino and thence the Po and into the Adriatic, and that on the west flowing into the Rhone and eventually the western Mediterranean.

On the Valais side of the pass, a little below the summit, a road leads off to the **Griessee**, an artificial lake dammed for HEP purposes, and fed by a glacier, the **Griesgletcher**. It is possible to drive a car nearly up to the dam, turning off the pass road at the second hairpin after descending the summit; there's a bus stop at this hairpin too. It takes around forty minutes to walk along the road to the dam from the pass summit. After crossing the dam wall on foot there's a path along the side of the lake which allows access to the grubby snout of the glacier (reached in around fifteen minutes), which feeds the lake directly amidst uncompromisingly bleak, high scenery.

From the bus stop and bend in the pass road there's a marked path over the **Griespass** which marks the border with Italy. Continuing by road into the Valais brings road

• SELECTED WALK •

THE STRADA DEGLI ALPI FROM PESCIÜM TO RONCO

3 hours 30 minutes • easy

This walk begins at Pesciüm, the middle station of the cable car which begins in Airolo. It then runs along the side of the Val Bedretto to Ronco, one of the villages in the valley. There are no steep ascents, and much of it keeps fairly level until the final section which runs gently down the valley side on a farm track – and it's a good walk to do outside the main summer season, when other walks in this region are still snowed up. It's also a good option in variable weather, when high altitude walks (such as those around Lago Ritòm) are less tempting. The highest part of the walk is Alpe Folcra (6,250ft/1,905m).

Most of the walk is on well-maintained farm tracks or other paths. It's easy to navigate and, although there's a maze of paths on this side of the Val Bedretto, it's impossible to get lost if you follow the red and white markers and keep taking the route marked 'Ronco' on signposts. The route is through forest and across farm and pastureland, with good views over the Val Bedretto in many places. After an hour and ten minutes walking from Pesciüm there's a path down to the village of Fontana (1hr), and around an hour later another path down to Bedretto (1hr). Ronco itself is a tiny hamlet in the Val Bedretto, with two restaurants and a bus down to Airolo every one or two hours.

travellers to the Rhone valley at **Ulrichen** after fifteen to twenty minutes (and lots more hairpins). From here it's possible to head west by rail or road routes to Brig, and then Sion and eventually Lake Geneva; or east, over the Furkapass (or through the Furka rail tunnel) to Andermatt, and then north towards central Switzerland or south over the Gotthard and back to Airolo.

AIROLO TO BIASCA – THE VALLE LEVENTINA

The stretch of road (and railway line) from Airolo to Biasca is one of the most scenic trunk routes in Europe and forms a wonderful approach to the more popular parts of the Ticino, which lie to the south. Major engineering works during the nineteenth century (on the Gotthard rail line) and the 1960s (on the motorway) ensure that travellers can breeze through this area with ease, taking only an hour (or even less) to reach Biasca from Airolo, in the process dropping around 2,600ft (800m) in *(cont'd on page 32)*

LAGO RITÒM TO PASSO DEL LUCOMAGNO (LUKMANIER PASS) VIA CAPANNA CADLIMO

6 hours • strenuous

This is one of the most spectacular walks in the Ticino, ascending from Lago Ritòm to Capanna Cadlimo, the highest mountain hut in the canton, and then heading through the bleak Val Cadlimo to the Lucomagno road pass above Olivone. It's tricky going in places, particularly around Capanna Cadlimo where there are some snow patches to cross, but the scenery is marvellous, particularly on the first part of the walk.

Lago Ritòm is set at an altitude of 6,070ft (1,850m), high above the Valle Leventina and reached by funicular from Piotta (see page 33). From the Lago Ritòm dam, head around the lake for around twenty minutes to **Alpe Ritom**, where there's a clearly marked path heading left: this is where the ascent starts, passing **Lago Tom** and reaching the smaller **Lago Taneda** in around an hour and fifteen minutes. From here there are great views back over Lago Ritòm and across to the high mountains of the Cristallina range, on the other side of the Valle Leventina.

The final steep bit comes immediately after Lago Taneda, as the path reaches **Lago Scuro** at the head of the Val Cadlimo. Although it's no longer steep from here onwards, it can be quite difficult, as the route crosses several snow patches between

The Capanna Cadlimo, the highest mountain hut in the Ticino

Above: Lago Ritòm is one of the most popular hiking areas in the Ticino

Right: Hiking routes from the Capanna Cadlimo

here and the **Capanna Cadlimo**, which is reached in around thirty minutes from Lago Scuro.

The capanna, set at 8,430ft (2,570m), offers spectacular mountain views if the weather is clear. There's basic cooked and cold food on offer here, and accommodation available in dormitories; phone ahead to book in advance ☎ (091) 869 1833. The

(cont'd overleaf)

• SELECTED WALK •

(cont'd from previous page)

capanna is open in July, August and September, and the first two weeks of October if the weather remains fine.

From the capanna it takes three hours to head down along the **Val Cadlimo** to the summit of the Passo del Lucomagno. The path is not difficult but the valley is not as interesting to walk in as the initial ascent from Lago Ritòm.

After around two hours the valley narrows and turns, and the final part, when the lake at the summit of the Passo del Lucomagno becomes visible, is tricky and takes a little less than an hour. Once by the lake — another artificial reservoir — follow the path round to the *ospizio* at the summit of the pass, where there's a good restaurant and dormitory accommodation available.

There are buses from here down to Biasca (1hr) from where there are trains back to Airolo (40min); check the bus timetable at the Capanna Cadlimo before leaving from there — the last bus down to Biasca normally leaves at around 5pm. The Passo del Lucomagno, the nearby walking centre of Olivone, and walks in this area, are described more fully in Chapter Two.

Other options

Instead of heading along the Val Cadlimo from the Capanna Cadlimo, as the walk above suggests, it is of course possible to simply descend back to Lago Ritòm: this takes around two hours.

There's an alternative path from Lago Ritòm to the Passo del Lucomagno which does not ascend as high as the route described in the walk above, passing the Capanna Cadagno (food and accommodation available) and crossing the Passo dell' Uomo; allow around four to five hours walking time from Lago Ritòm.

Lastly, there's a path from Capanna Cadlimo down to Airolo, which takes around four hours. A close study of the Gotthard 1:50,000 map shows still other available options.

altitude as the Ticino river cuts downwards through a series of impressive gorges.

Although there's plenty to see out of the window of a speeding car or train, and most visitors will just be content with this in their haste to head south for the lakes, there are some diversions along this route, principally among the villages which lie along the valley (or on sunny ledges high above it).

If exploring this area using public transport it's best to use the

Airolo-Biasca bus service, which is excellent. Buses link most of the places described below once an hour or more, and take around fifty minutes to complete the journey from Airolo to Biasca. Trains are faster, taking around forty minutes, but many of the villages in the valley have no station, and only the slowest trains stop at those which do.

Piotta: the funicular, and Lago Ritòm

The village of Piotta lies less than ten minutes by road east of Airolo. Hard up against the precipitous north wall of the valley is the lower station of one of the steepest funicular railways in the world, which ascends 2,625ft (800m) up the valley side at a maximum gradient of 88 per cent: basically a lift on rails.

There's a direct bus service to the lower station of the funicular from outside Airolo station once a day (line 600.53); otherwise, it's a walk of five to ten minutes from Ambrì-Piotta railway station, outside which the frequent buses on the Airolo-Biasca-Bellinzona route stop.

From the top station, **Piora**, there's a fabulous view of the Valle Leventina, with the trains travelling the Gotthard route resembling those on a model railway traversing an exaggeratedly steep papiermâché landscape. Piora station is a twenty-minute stroll along a paved level road from **Lago Ritòm**, an artificial lake dammed for hydro-electric purposes and set amidst bleak rocky slopes. There's a good restaurant at the far end of the dam wall, and, as the people in it togged up with rucksacks, stocking up with chocolate bars and

poring over maps would suggest, the place is the starting point for some seriously spectacular hikes in the surrounding area.

Piotta to Giornico

There's nothing really that special about **Quinto**, the next village in the valley beyond Piotta and the funicular. It's not on the main bus routes along the valley; to get there on foot from Piotta-Ambrì bus and rail station takes around thirty minutes, the marked path crossing an airfield runway which occupies the valley at this point.

Nonetheless, the main square is attractive, its cobbles sloping up to the church of St Peter and St Paul, the main focus of the village. The main body of the church is modern, but the six-storey Romanesque campanile is a much-admired and well-preserved example of Ticino architecture.

From the village, a road snakes up the valley sides to the villages of Catto and Lurengo, languishing on south-facing ledges of pastureland.

Seven minutes by bus beyond Piotta is **Rodi**, where there's a cable car up to Lago Tremorgio, a possible starting off point for difficult, high-altitude climbs. From the second bus station in the village (Rodi von Mentlen) there are four to six buses per day up to **Dalpe**; the road turning is just a short distance beyond Rodi.

There's a rather genteel hotel in Dalpe, next to the post office (in fact in Cornone, the northwards extension of the village) and although there's nothing specific to aim for, the place is pretty enough, and very quiet. From the road and

village there are excellent views along the Piumogna side valley and to Campo Tencia, at 10,080ft (3,072m) the highest mountain in the Ticino.

Dalpe is the starting point for some fairly heavy-going walks into the Campolungo range, which lies due south of the village; for an easier option, it takes around an hour and thirty minutes to walk from Dalpe down to Faido railway station in the valley, mostly through trees and across pastureland. About twenty to thirty minutes from Dalpe, on the marked track to Faido, there's a secluded swimming pool and restaurant-grotto at **Piana Selva**, which is linked by its own cable car to Faido. The cableway operates when required (and only when the grotto is open).

Faido is the main town in the Valle Leventina. Most trains stop here (the station is a short distance from the town centre) and the road passes right through the central square, its cafés shaded by trees. Just below the square (by the river, behind the Migros supermarket) is a private cable car to Piana Selva. The bottom station is unmanned: alert the operator by pressing the button, and pay at the top.

Just over 4 miles (7km) beyond Faido the Ticino river suddenly drops down steeply, cutting a narrow gash through the cliffs and presenting transport engineers with a problem. The builders of the railway drilled curving tunnels through the rock so that the tracks could spiral downwards – the classic Alpine solution to gaining or losing height over a short distance.

Next to the spirals, the main motorway crosses the valley on an enormously high concrete viaduct, which rail travellers see three times as they spiral downwards. A short distance beyond the gorge the valley opens out at Giornico, easily the most interesting and attractive settlement in the Valle Leventina.

Giornico

With the main Gotthard motorway sheltered from view (and mercifully out of earshot) behind a steep cliff, Giornico, an ancient crossing point of the packhorse track which ran up the valley towards the Gotthard, is a delightfully quiet and picturesque place, not really noticed by most travellers. The railway station is closed, but buses still stop on the old road which passes along the east side of the valley at this point.

From here, cross the river to the **church of San Nicolao**, which is surrounded by small private vineyards and nestles right next to the railway lines. Next door (slightly further on) is a much more modern church, which is not particularly exciting.

Five minutes away on foot from the church of San Nicolao is another ancient church, the **Chapel of Santa Maria of the Castle**, whose campanile overlooks the village from atop a rocky bluff. There are more medieval wall paintings here, plus scant remains of a castle, of which the church was once a part.

Back in the village, on the other side of the river, a steeply sloping road (leading off the main road by a Hyundai garage) leads to the **Casa Stanga**, once the house of a sixteenth-century noble family, now the **Folk Museum** of the Valle Leventina. It's only open on Sunday afternoons, but at other times the Osteria Giornico, on the main road, will supply the key to the front door.

Not far from here, across two ancient arched bridges which span the two channels of the Ticino river, is a nice riverside café, the Grotto dei due Ponti.

Nearly 6 miles (9km) beyond Giornico the valley really opens up at **Biasca**, the first of a number of industrial towns which have grown up along the Ticino valley between Giornico and Lake Maggiore. All the places described in the preceding section can easily be visited from Biasca, the access point for Olivone and the beautiful Val Blenio, which along with Biasca itself are described in the next chapter.

Church of San Nicolao

San Nicolao, with its fine Romanesque features, is a place of architectural pilgrimage in the valley. It was built in the twelfth century and was probably once part of a monastery. Inside, the tiny, high-set windows make the place gloomy and mysterious, a mood accentuated by the curious arrangement of an open crypt at the far end, and by the remains of fading medieval wall paintings.

PLACES TO VISIT

The Hospice Fort Museum
Airolo
Open: June-October, daily,
9am-6pm. ☎ (091) 869 1430

**The National Museum
of St Gotthard**
St Gotthard Pass
Open: June-October, daily,
9am-6pm. ☎ (091) 869 1525

Casa Stanga
Giornico
Open: Sunday afternoons, 2-5pm.
Key available at other times from
Ospizio Giornico on main road.

HOTELS

Tourist offices can supply the brochure *Alto Ticino: Hotels* which gives
full details of all accommodation possibilities in this part of the Ticino:
hotels, holiday flats, mountain huts, camping, group accommodation
and restaurants with rooms. Some possibilities include:

Airolo

*** Albergo Motta
☎ (091) 869 2211,
Fax (091) 869 2225
www.albergo-motta.ch

*** Forni
Via Stazione
☎ (091) 869 1270,
Fax (091) 869 1523
e-mail info@forni.ch
Family-run hotel opposite
Airolo station.

** Des Alpes
Via Stazione
☎ (091) 869 1715,
Fax (091) 869 1723
Slightly less pricey, also
opposite Airolo station.

* Osteria Helvetia
Via Stazione
☎ (091) 869 1515
Small hotel, one of the
cheapest in Airolo; just
up from station.

* Pesciüm Hotel
*Next to top station of
funicular from Airolo*
☎ (091) 869 2618,
Fax (091) 869 2812
5,000ft (1,500m) in altitude;
surprisingly inexpensive; of
most interest to skiers.

Ambrì

Monte Pettine
☎ (091) 868 1124,
Fax (091) 868 1872

Hotel Stazione
☎ (091) 868 1232

Other places

* All'Acqua Hotel
All'Acqua
☎ (091) 869 1185
Cheap hotel in tiny village
twenty-five minutes by road west
of Airolo; five buses per day.

* Orelli Hotel
Bedretto
☎ (091) 869 1140,
Fax (091) 869 2412
Family-run hotel in tiny village
twenty minutes by road west
of Airolo; five buses per day.

** Tre Cervi
Campello
☎ (091) 866 2661
Good hotel in tiny village above
Faido; very limited bus service.

** Stella Alpina
Ronco
☎ (091) 869 1714
Nice hotel with family rooms
in tiny village in Val Bedretto;
limited bus links.

** Ospizo San Gottardo
Summit of St Gotthard Pass
☎ (091) 869 1235,
Fax (091) 869 1811
Hotel at the summit
of the pass.

PUBLIC TRANSPORT

Trains

Hourly service Airolo-Faido-Biasca (40min). Most express and
international trains run from Bellinzona through the Gotthard without
stopping at stations in this chapter. Times by direct train from Airolo:
Chiasso 1hr 45min; Lugano 1hr 20min; Bellinzona 55min; Zurich 1hr
30min; Luzern 1hr 20min; Basel 2hr 30min.

Buses

Hourly service **Airolo-Ambrì-Rodi-Faido-Lavorgo-Giornico-Biasca-
Bellinzona** (75min).

Airolo-St Gotthard-Andermatt: 3 daily (53min), during summer only.

Airolo-All'Acqua: 4-7 per day (24min). Airolo-Ronco: 4-5 per day
(15min).

TOURIST OFFICE

Airolo ☎ (091) 869 1533

*T*he Val Blenio is a principal tributary valley of the Valle Leventina, and is a beautiful retreat from the busyness of Bellinzona and the southern Ticino. At its northern end, cradled in a bowl surrounded by high peaks, is Olivone, an important walking centre. Picturesque villages such as Torre and Prugiasco line the Brenno river as it runs down from here to join the Ticino at Biasca, the main point of entry to the valley from the Valle Leventina.

Beyond Olivone is the **Passo del Lucomagno**, open only a few months of each year, which provides road access to **Disentis**, on the main Chur-Andermatt-Brig road. There's skiing at Bassa di Nara and Leontica, half-way between Biasca and Olivone, but it's walking for which this area is best known. There are no rail connections, but the bus service is excellent, with regular services between Biasca and Olivone taking thirty-five to fifty-five minutes (depending on the route), with some buses continuing on to Disentis if the pass is open.

BIASCA

Biasca, the gateway to the Val Blenio and situated at its confluence with the Valle Leventina, is an uninspiring place. The main Gotthard motorway swings west to by-pass the town. The approach from the south, along the adjacent main road and railway, takes travellers past a shabby string of light industrial units, warehouses and unappealing apartment blocks painted dull shades of grey and green before the centre of town is reached.

The church of San Pietro in Biasca

The railway station, overlooked by a waterfall which splashes down the vertical slopes immediately above the platforms, is the town's central point of reference. Buses south to Bellinzona, north-west to the Gotthard and north up the Val Blenio to Olivone all depart from outside the station entrance. The fastest trains don't stop here, but Biasca is still a reasonably good transport hub. Its hotels, lining the road opposite the station, are good value as Biasca is not a particularly popular place to stay.

Biasca's position at the meeting point of two pass routes – the St Gotthard and the Passo del Lucomagno – has assured it a strategic importance and a commercial role in the past, but this has given way to fairly ordinary agricultural and industrial functions today. Gneiss, a form of granite stone which breaks along cleavage lines like slate, is quarried here, and can be seen covering the roofs of many Ticino houses. Figs, vines and walnuts are cultivated on land which isn't too steep or otherwise occupied by buildings. Warehouses, distribution depots and factories have taken advantage of the town's centrality in the Ticino and its easy access to the Blenio and Leventina valleys. Few tourists come here, and those that do are usually only passing through.

If you're hanging around in Biasca between transport connections, then the only things to see are its two **churches**, which overlook the confluence of the Val Blenio and the Valle Leventina, on the east side of the town. They are reached by turning right out of the station and heading through the underpass, which dives beneath the railway lines as they curve west. After ten minutes you will reach the first church, a squat, octagonal structure whose interior is surprisingly, and defiantly, modern and lacking in charm. Less than ten minutes' walk up the hillside is the smaller church of San Pietro, whose slim pointed tower is photogenically framed by the mountains to the north. The building is unfortunately locked most of the time, but its setting, amidst vineyards and commanding fine views of the Valle Leventina, is worth making the short detour for.

BIASCA TO THE PASSO DEL LUCOMAGNO, VIA OLIVONE

Immediately north of Biasca, on the right hand side, is the **Buzza di Biasca**, the remains (in the form of rock deposits strewn across the valley) of a landslide which occurred in 1512. The collapsed material dammed up the river and created a temporary lake in the valley here, whose waters broke through the dam in 1514, causing a devastating flood which reached as far south as Lake Maggiore.

After the Buzza di Biasca there is a left-hand turning for Semione, with the main road continuing on to Malvaglia; some Biasca-Olivone buses take the Semione route but most pass along the main road through Malvaglia.

Malvaglia and Semione

Malvaglia, 3.7 miles (6km) north of Biasca, occupies the flat valley floor at the point where it begins to narrow, and the road begins to climb. It's not a particularly pretty place, but the church, situated just off the main road to the right, is worth a brief look: it's a Romanesque structure, whose bell-tower is the tallest – and one of the most finely fashioned – in the Ticino.

Rising up the steep slopes of the valley side opposite Malvaglia, **Semione** is far more appealing, its houses laid out along narrow streets which snake up towards upland pastures. The distinctive church tower can be seen clearly from Malvaglia. On a street above the church is the **Casa San Carlo**

which houses a collection of minerals from the region, and fossils from the Jura mountains in north-western Switzerland; the museum is signposted from the northern end of the village.

A little further north of Semione, on a minor road linking the village with **Rongie** (at the northern end of Malvaglia), the castle of **Serravalle** sits on a bluff overlooking the point where the valley begins to narrow. It's a picturesque ruin, reached by a three-minute stroll up a steep track which begins next to a modern farm building. Buses travelling through Malvaglia will stop next at Rongie, from where it's a ten minute walk to Serravalle.

Acquarossa and Leontica

Nearly 4 miles (6km) beyond Malvaglia is **Acquarossa**, an unremarkable place which gives access to the main walking area of the central Val Blenio; the valley's main skiing areas are situated above Acquarossa, too.

Although buses running between Biasca and Olivone stop in the centre of Acquarossa, the village of **Leontica**, twenty minutes away by road, is a better starting point for walks. Seven buses per day run from Acquarossa to Leontica, but if there's no bus then it takes an hour of steep, uphill walking to reach the latter settlement, up the road or a marked path. The path up to Leontica from Prugiasco, just beyond Acquarossa, takes longer, but is more interesting, passing the **church of San Carlo di Negrentino** (*see* page 44).

At Leontica (2,870ft/875m) is the lower station of a two-stage

Serravalle Castle

The castle was founded in the late twelfth century by the local Lombard nobility and was besieged in 1176 by the Emperor Frederick Barbarossa. In later medieval times it became a residence of the Orellisi dynasty of Locarno before falling into the hands of a feudal dynasty loyal to the Duke of Milan. The castle was destroyed in 1402 during a popular rebellion in the valley which unseated Taddeo de Pepoli, the last feudal overlord, and has been in ruins ever since.

The ruins of
Serravalle Castle

Cascata Sta.
Petronilla

Winter near Bassa di Nara, accessible by chairlift and the main
skiing area of the Val Blenio

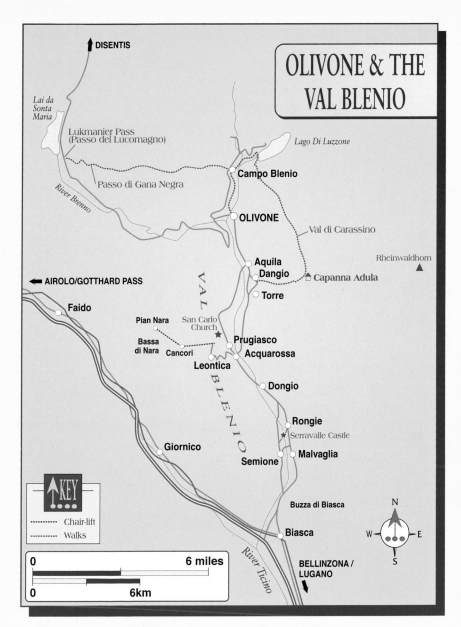

OLIVONE & THE VAL BLENIO

DISENTIS

Lai da Sonta Maria

Lukmanier Pass (Passo del Lucomagno)

Lago Di Luzzone

Campo Blenio

River Brenno

Passo di Gana Negra

OLIVONE

Val di Carassino

AIROLO/GOTTHARD PASS

Aquila

Dangio

Rheinwaldhorn

Capanna Adula

VAL

Torre

Faido

Pian Nara

San Carlo Church

Bassa di Nara

Cancori

Prugiasco

Acquarossa

Leontica

BLENIO

Dongio

Rongie

Serravalle Castle

Giornico

Semione

Malvaglia

KEY

···· Chair-lift

···· Walks

Buzza di Biasca

N

Biasca

W   E

S

0   6 miles

0   6km

River Ticino

BELLINZONA / LUGANO

cableway up to **Pian Nara** (6,365ft/1,940m) via Cancorì (4,790ft/1,460m). Pian Nara lies just below the **Bassa di Nara**, a pass that can be reached in under an hour from the top of the chairlift. From here walkers can drop down to a number of places in the Valle Leventina on any number of paths; the most obvious place to head for is Faido, which has a railway station. Otherwise, it's a three-hour walk from Bassa di Nara back down to Acquarossa via San Carlo church. There are ski grounds around Bassa di Nara, with snow here lasting well into May.

The church of San Carlo di Negrentino

This church, which occupies a sunny area of pastureland just below Leontica village, is one of the most important Romanesque buildings in Switzerland. Founded in the early eleventh century and dedicated to St Ambrose, it's a tiny, two-aisle structure, whose interior is adorned with frescoes, the oldest of which (dated to around 1050) depicts the ascension of Christ amongst the Apostles.

The artist is thought to have been a wandering Milanese painter of frescoes; his work (much of it now lost) is also thought to adorn other churches in this part of the southern Alps – as artists working at that time were nomadic, travelling from commission to commission. In the oldest nave, at the apse end of the north wall, are later paintings, dating from the fifteenth and early sixteenth centuries and also by wandering Milanese fresco artists.

The church is situated on a marked path which runs from the car park for the lower chairlift station at Leontica, to the Passo del Nara bar/restaurant in Prugiasco, two-thirds of a mile (1km) north of Acquarossa on the road which runs along the western side of the valley. It's a ten minute walk down to the church from the car park (the path crosses a narrow gorge via a footbridge) or a forty to fifty minute walk up from Prugiasco, across meadowland. The church is locked, but restaurants in Leontica and Prugiasco (including the Passo del Nara bar) should be able to lend you a key.

Northern Val Blenio – Dangio and Olivone

Beyond Acquarossa the valley narrows still further and settlement becomes more scattered. **Dangio**, half way between Acquarossa and Olivone, is easily the most picturesque village in the Val Blenio. There's a modern by-pass, which crosses a tributary of the Brenno on an impressive single-span bridge, but there's also a road through Dangio itself which passes the shuttered and derelict Cima-Norma chocolate factory before entering the main part of the village. Here, the main points of interest (and activity) are the road-side cafés, which face south to soak up the sun.

Both Dangio and **Aquila**, the next village on along the valley, were manufacturing chocolate as long ago as the seventeenth century, and emigrants from this area took chocolate-making crafts to Spain, France, England and even – it is thought – Constantinople. The factory in Dangio closed in 1966, its location too remote for modern methods of chocolate making. However, locals believe that this area of the Val Blenio has contributed to the international fame of

Swiss chocolate, which may be one reason why the factory has been left there, still bearing the name of the company.

Olivone, another 2 miles (3km) on from Dangio, is largely a modern settlement, though attractively situated in a natural sun-trap where the main road in the valley swings west. Sosto, a distinctively-shaped, bulky pyramidal peak, overlooks the village to the north and is a focal point of the topography of the Val Blenio.

The village originally grew up as a transit station on the pass; nowadays it's primarily a walking centre, the starting point for a number of high-altitude and difficult walks. The only specific thing to see in the village is the **San Martino Museum** (signposted), a cultural record of the Blenio valley, with furniture, costumes, and religious artefacts from the church of Olivone on display. The church is in fact next door, and you may need to borrow the key to the museum from the parsonage.

Olivone to Disentis – the Passo del Lucomagno

Beyond Olivone the road ascends a series of broad loops as it enters the **Valle Santa Maria**. There are fine views (look behind you) over Olivone and beyond to the mountains on the Ticino-Grisons border, of which Rheinwaldhorn (11,160ft/3,402m) is the highest. The road journey to the summit of the **Passo del Lucomagno** (Lukmanier Pass) is an easy one. The road is not cleared in winter (it is closed for maybe five months of the year beyond Olivone) and in summer is served by around three buses a day, which carry on from the pass to the mountain town of Disentis in the Grisons, serving the Biasca-Olivone-Disentis route. At the summit of the pass next to a small lake and set amid bleak, rocky scenery, is an *ospizio*, which offers basic rooms and a restaurant. Buses stop outside.

PASSO DEL LUCOMAGNO TO OLIVONE, VIA CAMPO BLENIO

6 hours • quite strenuous

This is a fairly strenuous walk that covers some high, bleak mountain scenery around the Passo del Lucomagno and then descends through forests to the ski resort of Campo Blenio, and thence to Olivone.

The path is clearly signposted from the summit of the Passo del Lucomagno. It's a steady climb of around sixty to ninety minutes up to the summit of the Passo di Gana Negra, involving an ascent of around 1,640ft (500m). The scenery around the top of the pass is a little surreal, consisting of a huge sea of boulders of different sizes, set amid a boggy landscape and dwarfed by steep peaks. There are patches of snow on the slopes just above the pass all year round, feeding cascading waterfalls.

From the summit of the pass the path descends steadily, eventually passing (after around seventy-five minutes) a

Piana di Dongio

huge, V-shaped cowshed (the farmers there don't mind being asked for water). Beyond the cowshed there is a motorable track down to Campo Blenio, which eventually becomes a tarred road; there are also paths through the woods down to Campo Blenio, which don't follow motorable roads. Either way is signposted and easy to follow; you'll reach Campo Blenio in around two hours.

Campo Blenio

Campo Blenio is a small ski resort and agricultural village set in fine scenery and overlooked from a great height by the dam on the **Lago di Luzzone**, which you'll see as you come down from the pass. There are two restaurants in the village, both of which offer rooms. You'll pass by one of them, the Genziana, if you keep following the signs to Olivone.

Campo Blenio and Olivone are linked by a very limited bus service (around two or three buses per day). It takes just less than one hour to carry on from Campo Blenio to Olivone, following the road to begin with, then taking a left (just as the road enters a tunnel) and following a

(cont'd overleaf)

Campo Blenio and Olivone are linked by a path which runs along this impressive gorge

• SELECTED WALKS •

(cont'd from previous page)

gorge, with the path clinging to the overhanging cliffs in spectacular fashion. The path brings you to the post office (and adjacent hotel/restaurant) in the centre of Olivone, by the bus stop on the Biasca-Olivone- Passo del Lucomagno route.

VAL DI CARASSINO – A CIRCULAR ROUTE FROM DANGIO

8-9 hours • strenuous

A full day's hiking, starting at the village of Dangio, rising up 3,940ft (1,200m) to **Capanna Adula**, then along the Val di Carassino to the Lago di Luzzone dam, before finally descending to Campo Blenio.

From Dangio follow the red trail that begins by the small church just above the cable-car station, which will eventually lead you up to a rough roadtrack. For some strange reason the red markers disappear along here, but follow it up to the village of Soi, a steady, but gentle climb (if the stream is on your right then you're on the right track).

From Soi the red markers make a welcome reappearance, directing you first up to the small settlement of Jra and then onto the ascent proper – it's a steep climb but the path is well-made and the views fantastic. The entire trek from Dangio up to the refreshment hut Capanna Adula should be accomplishable in around about four hours.

From here the walk along the beautiful Val di Carassino is decidedly less arduous – it's a long one undoubtedly, but very relaxing and once the stream has formed itself into a small lake you're very much on the home straight. Just beyond the path branches, so you can either head down to Olivone (1hr 50min), or treat yourself to a visit to the truly awe-inspiring Lago di Luzzone dam on the way to Campo Blenio.

The official path to Campo Blenio actually takes you along the top of the dam and those of a nervous disposition may feel the need to bend their knees and cling desperately to the railing when looking down the sheer drop (N.B. abseiling is expressly prohibited). The final descent into Campo Blenio takes no more than an hour and the entire journey from Capanna Adula should be no more than five hours in total.

From Campo Blenio see notes on previous walk..

PLACES TO VISIT

Serravalle Castle
Access at any time.

Fossil Museum, Semione

Olivone Museum
Open: Easter-October by appointment only. ☎ (091) 870 1261

ACCOMMODATION

Biasca

*** **Al Giardinetto**
Via Pini 21
☎ (091) 862 1771, Fax (091) 862 2359,
e-mail info@algiardinetto.ch
Well appointed hotel in Biasca.

** **Posta**
Via Bellinzona, ☎/Fax (091) 862 212
Cheaper hotel, right opposite the station.

* **Stazione**
Via Bellinzona, ☎ (091) 862 2725
Another, plainer, hotel opposite the station.

* **Alloggio Juliana**
Via Chiasso 14, ☎ (091) 862 2709
Cheap hotel on the road leading south from Biasca.

Dongio

* **Della Piazza**
Via Cantonale, ☎ (091) 871 2898
Inexpensive family-run hotel.

Olivone

*** **Olivone e Posta**
Via Lucomagno, ☎ (091) 872 1366,
Fax (091) 872 2256
Very well appointed hotel right in the centre of Olivone.

** **San Martino**
☎ (091) 872 1521, Fax (091) 872 2662
Medium-range accommodation in the centre of the village.

* **Osteria Centrale**
Via alla Chiesa, ☎ (091) 872 1107
Simple hotel, the cheapest in Olivone.

Campo Blenio

Genziana
☎ (091) 872 1193/2598
Friendly, inexpensive small timber-built lodgings, overlooking the stream on the road to Olivone.

PUBLIC TRANSPORT

Biasca-Olivone: up to 11 buses per day (40min).

Olivone-Passo del Lucomagno summit: 3 buses per day in summer (20min).

Acquarossa-Leontica: 3-7 buses per day (10-20min).

Olivone-Campo Blenio: 1-5 buses per day (10min).

Biasca-Bellinzona: up to 3 trains or buses per hour (15min).

Biasca-Airolo: 1 train per hour (25min).

Biasca-Lugano: 1 train per hour (50min).

TOURIST OFFICES

Biasca ☎ (091) 862 3327

Acquarossa ☎ (091) 871 1765

Collegiata Church, Bellinzona, overlooked by Castello di Monteballo

*B*ellinzona is the cantonal capital of the Ticino and has a number of sights of historical interest. Although it's rather a sterile town it's worth a brief visit, and because Bellinzona lies at the geographical centre of the canton, it makes an excellent base for seeing the whole region described in this book. More appealing is the Valle Mesolcina, an attractive valley running between Bellinzona and the Passo del San Bernardino, giving access to fine scenery and good opportunities for walking, skiing and touring.

BELLINZONA

Bellinzona seems jealous of Lugano and Locarno. The cantonal capital gets overlooked by tourists in favour of the lakeside cities, which are more attractively situated, better known, and have a far more varied cultural and artistic life than Bellinzona.

The tourist brochures and other publications issued by the city authorities admit this, one going so far as to say that "Bellinzona is little known by tourists and underrated by the people of Ticino themselves, used to, as they have always been, identifying it with the windy administrative cantonal centre". However, the brochure goes on to say that Bellinzona is at last "shedding its image of sleepy provincial backwater and emerging with renewed vitality".

Perhaps things are livelier in Bellinzona than they used to be, but there is no point pretending that the city doesn't lose out to the lakeside resorts on most counts. Its situation is not as impressive, there is of course no lake, less in the way of cultural life and the place is given over to living and working, rather than relaxing and soaking up views and the sunshine.

Nevertheless, it's equally important not to overlook the more worthwhile aspects of the city – there's a fair bit to see here, including three medieval castles (*see* page 54) which overlook the well-preserved centre and the Saturday market, held in the Old Town (the liveliest in the canton). There are also far fewer visitors here than by the lakes, making the place quieter, less expensive and more genuinely Swiss. Perhaps the greatest advantage of Bellinzona, as far as visitors are concerned, is its location at the heart of the Ticino and the easy access to all places described in this book.

Bellinzona is an important road and rail junction and it's impossible to spend much time in the Ticino without at least passing through. Andermatt, just beyond the top of the St Gotthard Pass, is 40 miles (64km) away by motorway, and Lugano and Locarno are both less than 15 miles (25km) away heading in the opposite direction. Trains on the main rail route from Basel to Milan stop here: Lugano and Locarno are both less than thirty minutes away, Milan around ninety minutes away, and Airolo, at the head of the Gotthard valley, forty-five minutes away.

Some history

Three important trans-Alpine routes converge in the Ticino valley – the St Gotthard, the San Bernardino, and the Lucomagno – and southerly access to all three of them is controlled by Bellinzona, giving the city immense strategic importance (and accounting for the fact that there are three castles here).

The city came under Roman rule between 30BC and 450AD and was ruled in medieval times by Milanese dynasties, the Viscontis and then the Sforzas. The castles and the double circuit of walls were built in the late fifteenth century by the Sforzas. By 1503 the Swiss Confederates had established a governor's office in the city, an event which eventually resulted in the Ticino becoming a Swiss canton in 1803. Bellinzona has been cantonal capital since 1878, and is now an important educational, administrative, industrial and commercial centre.

If you want to see a lot of the Ticino and don't want to suffer the high costs and visitor numbers of the lakeside resorts, then Bellinzona is probably the best place to stay.

The Old Town

At the heart of medieval Bellinzona are two adjacent, irregularly shaped and arcaded squares, the **Piazza Nosetto** and the **Piazza Collegiata**, which are situated 656yd (600m) south-west of the railway station along the Viale

Bellinzona Market

The Saturday morning market, which occupies the southern end of the Viale Stazione and the area around the two central squares, is the highlight of Bellinzona. It's the largest of its kind in the Ticino and puts a neat dent in the otherwise rather sterile and fussily-ordered atmosphere of the city centre.

To the accompaniment of street music – anything from 'oom-pah' bands to more solitary banjo or guitar acts – shoppers browse amongst the videos, CDs, books, clothes, computer gear, knick-knacks and kitsch. Of more interest to visitors is the local produce on sale – this is an excellent place to buy cheese, meats, wine and honey, with goods often simply packaged and sold by the farmers who produce them.

Stazione. Both are intimate spaces, neither really suggesting Bellinzona's current size or importance, and they occasionally get clogged with people. Lined with flash boutiques and jewellery shops, things are liveliest here on Saturday mornings when the city plays host to the busiest street market in the Ticino.

On the more northerly of the two squares is the **Collegiata Church of SS Pietro and Stefano**, the largest in Bellinzona, whose flight of stone steps form the city's main gathering and meeting point. Founded in 1424, it was rebuilt in 1517 by the architect Tomaso Rodari, who at that time was master builder of Como Cathedral. The rich Baroque exterior and façade were added in the seventeenth and eighteenth centuries. It's an airy, spacious building, rather swamped by Baroque effusiveness, and mostly silent. The representation of the crucifixion above the high altar, dated to 1658, is thought to be by Tintoretto.

Ravecchia

Around 875yd (800m) south of the main town centre, along the Via Lugano which leads off from the Piazza Nosetto, is a clutch of buildings, including two churches and an art gallery, which form the focal point of the district of Ravecchia.

The **Villa dei Cedri**, an elegant villa in its own secluded garden, contains an art gallery with paintings by nineteenth and twentieth century Swiss and Italian artists.

Across the quiet square from here is the **Chiesa San Biagio**, a squat, Romanesque building whose

Bellinzona's three castles

As far as visitors are concerned, the main feature of Bellinzona are its three medieval castles – the most distinctive in the Ticino. Their presence gives an idea of the strategic significance of the town and its main historical role, controlling access to three important passes over the Alps.

Castelgrande

Castelgrande is the oldest and most central of the three, built over the site of a Roman fort and located right in the centre of Bellinzona. The best way of reaching it is to follow the narrow, signposted lane which leads off from the triangular Piazza Collegiata (opposite the church).

The castle has suffered some fairly indiscreet modern additions this century and is not particularly pretty, either from afar or close up. The two square towers, the Torre Negra and the Torre Bianca, are the oldest remaining parts and date from the fourteenth century. The views from the ramparts are good – there's a small outdoor café which overlooks the oldest part of the town centre. However, the collections inside are not terribly enticing, consisting of a historical museum (coins and other artefacts), a cinema programme about the history of Bellinzona (in Italian only) and a room for temporary art exhibitions.

Castello di Montebello

The Castello di Montebello, reached by a flight of stone steps that lead off from behind the Collegiata Church, is rather more attractive, with carefully-tended lawns and courtyards. Parts of the central keep date again from the fourteenth century; unfortunately the historical and archaeological collections inside don't hold much interest unless you read Italian and/or have a good working knowledge and interest in Roman and medieval Ticino history.

original medieval appearance was restored in 1914. The fresco on the outside wall, above and to the left of the front door, dates from the end of the fourteenth century and is a giant portrait of St Christopher. Inside there are more murals dating from around the same era, but as usual the door will probably be locked and you are unlikely to be able to see them.

Across the railway lines, around 220yd (200m) to the west, is the **Chiesa Santa Maria delle Grazie**, a convent church founded around 1480 and associated with the Franciscan order. The church is famed for its interior wall frescoes, painted between 1495 and 1505 by an unknown Lombard artist, which have been undergoing extensive restoration. The immaculately detailed and vivid designs depict the life of Christ and are centred on a moving representation of the Crucifixion. They are well worth trying to see, although restoration work may mean that all or part of the church is closed off at any one time.

Castelgrande

Castello di Sasso Corbaro

A good forty minute walk up from Castello di Montebello is the
Castello di Sasso Corbaro. The castle was built in six months, in 1479,
to reinforce the defences of the Ticino valley after the Battle of
Giornico, in which the Milanese, until then the overlords of the Ticino,
were defeated by the Swiss Confederation.

It's much smaller than the other two castles, consisting of a solid,
high-walled square keep. There's a small museum of Ticino arts, crafts
and costumes, which keeps rather erratic opening hours, and a rather
expensive restaurant in the keep.

Monte Carasso and walks near Bellinzona

An aerial cableway which starts
next to the main Bellinzona-
Locarno road at Monte Carasso
(1 mile/2km west of the city
centre) and ascends to **Mornera**,
provides access for walks close to
Bellinzona. From the top station,
where whitewashed villas poke
out from among clumps of pine
trees, it's possible to walk back
down to Monte Carasso (2 hrs),
or along the valley sides to **Baltico**
(1 hr).

Baltico is the top station of another cableway, the lower station
of which is at Galbisio, on the west
bank of the Ticino river just north
of Bellinzona. Both these walks are
straightforward and easy; more
ambitious walkers will want to
head up from Mornera to Alpe
Albagno and even further, into the
Locarno valleys which lie to the
west of here.

VALLE MESOLCINA – BELLINZONA TO THE PASSO DEL SAN BERNARDINO

The Valle Mesolcina is a deep-sided valley whose precipitous sides are punctuated by a number of spectacular waterfalls. It lies north-east of Bellinzona and links the town with the Passo del San Bernardino, which carries road traffic from the Ticino into north-eastern Switzerland and beyond. It's not actually a part of Canton Ticino – very shortly after leaving Bellinzona there is a cantonal boundary post which marks the fact that you are entering Canton Grisons (or Graubünden), the largest in Switzerland. Most of the Grisons is German or Romansch-speaking, but the inhabitants of the Mesolcina valley speak Italian, and culturally, historically and architecturally the area has more in common with the Ticino than with the rest of the canton, which is why it is covered in this book.

Many visitors to the Ticino travel through the Mesolcina valley – it's a major traffic artery – but few seem to make it a destination in itself. The most obvious points to aim for are at the head of the valley: the pass itself, the town of San Bernardino, which is a large walking and skiing centre, and the picturesque village of Mesocco, the site of one of the most dramatically-situated ruined castles in the country.

The only access to the valley is by road. The old road and the modern (single-lane) motorway both compete for space on the narrow valley floor as far as San Bernardino, where the former climbs up to the Pass, while the latter plunges into a tunnel through the mountain. At frequent points along the valley it is possible to join or rejoin the motorway. There are frequent buses between Bellinzona and San Bernardino, using both the motorway and the old road, some of which carry on through the tunnel to Chur (Coira in Italian), the main centre of the Grisons.

The Ferrovia Mesolcinese operates a very limited rail service (currently running trains on only a few Sundays in summer) between Castione, immediately north of Bellinzona, and Cama, a short distance along the valley. Timetables can be picked up from tourist offices and Bellinzona station, although it's difficult to see what use car-less tourists will make of this line.

This rail line, which originally reached as far up the valley as Mesocco, was closed in 1972, but the Castione-Cama section was re-opened in 1995. Parts of the former track-bed beyond Cama have been turned into a footpath, with dramatically-situated bridges and cuttings still preserved in a number of places.

Bellinzona to Mesocco

The turning for both San Bernardino roads lies a short distance to the north of Bellinzona. The valley is fairly broad and flat as far as **Roveredo**, where the **Centro Sportivo Vera** is an excellent base for this region if you intend to camp. There's open-air swimming, tennis, hang-gliding, and even archery, all located at the Centro which caters particularly for families. Just beyond Roveredo is the turning for the Val Calanca, a peaceful and secluded side-valley of the Mesolcina.

Beyond Roveredo the valley narrows and the road begins to climb. The valley sides soon become unusually precipitous, with villages and farms clinging to the sides where they can. There are a number of waterfalls which cascade down the cliffs, the most spectacular, beside the old road half-way between Cabbiolo and Soazza, is the **Boffalora Cascade**.

Soazza is an attractive village, its church dramatically perched on a steep-sided bluff overlooking the valley. But it's the next village further on, **Mesocco**, which commands most attention. Immediately before the roads enter the village, the sombre-hued walls of the **Castello di Mesocco** rise up from the deep, craggy valley of the River Moesa, which is here at its deepest point.

The village of Mesocco is the most attractive in the valley. The main road goes under part of the village into a tunnel, but the continuous noise of traffic makes it hard to forget it's there. Buses stop next to the old station, disused for nearly thirty years but still with rails visibly embedded in the tarmac next to the former platforms. The marked path from here to the castle partly follows the course of the old railway.

San Bernardino village

The journey by road from Mesocco up to San Bernardino is one of the most spectacular in the Ticino. The road crosses a couple of impressive arched bridges just above Mesocco, passes through a couple of tunnels and then past a small artificial lake before reaching San Bernardino and the tunnel entrance.

In contrast to Mesocco, **San Bernardino** is an ugly place, a collection of modern hotel and

(cont'd on page 60)

Castello di Mesocco

The castle's ruined state adds to its allure, the crumbling walls seem almost to be part of the sheer granite cliffs on which they were built. In early medieval times the castle was a place of refuge for the valley's people; later on in the twelfth century the local magnates, the Counts Sax, extended and strengthened it. There's not much to see inside the walls nowadays save precipitous drops and weed-infested ramparts, but it's the location atop a vertical-sided gorge which makes it worth visiting.

On the way up to the castle is the twelfth-century **church of Santa Maria al Castello**, distinguished by a huge fresco of St Christopher on its exterior wall and adorned with well preserved fifteenth-century paintings inside (pick up the key from restaurants in the village).

The Saturday morning market in Bellinzona is the busiest in the Ticino

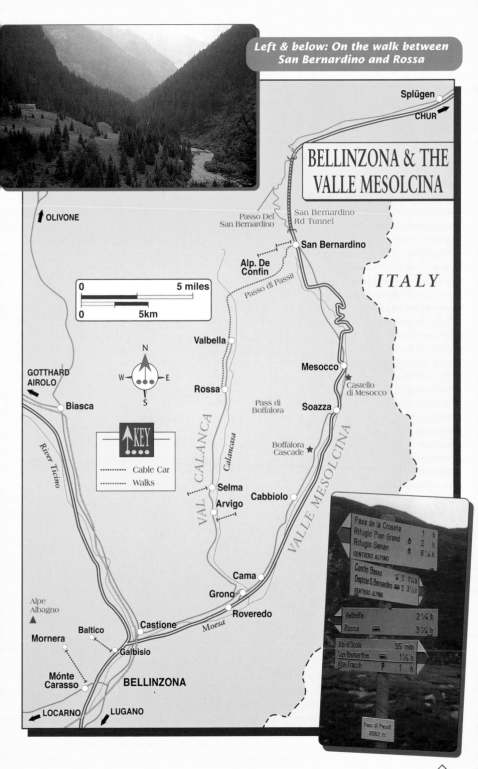

Left & below: On the walk between San Bernardino and Rossa

BELLINZONA & THE VALLE MESOLCINA

Splügen

CHUR

Passo Del San Bernardino

San Bernardino Rd Tunnel

San Bernardino

Alp. De Confin

ITALY

Passo di Passit

OLIVONE

Valbella

Mesocco

Castello di Mesocco

Rossa

Pass di Boffalora

Soazza

GOTTHARD AIROLO

Biasca

Boffalora Cascade

River Ticino

VAL CALANCA

Calancasa

VALLE MESOLCINA

KEY

.... Cable Car
.... Walks

Selma

Cabbiolo

Arvigo

Cama

Grono

Roveredo

Moesa

Alpe Albagno

Baltico

Castione

Mornera

Galbisio

Mónte Carasso

BELLINZONA

LOCARNO   LUGANO

| 0 | | 5 miles |
| 0 | | 5km |

N
W   E
S

Pass de la Cruseta   1 h
Rifugio Pian Grand   2 h
Rifugio Ganan   6¼ h
SENTIERO ALPINO

Confin Basso   1¼ h
Ospizio S.Bernardino   3½ h
SENTIERO ALPINO

Valbella   2¼ h
Rossa   3¼ h

Alp di Dcola   35 min
San Bernardino   1½ h
Alpe Fracch   P   1 h

Pass di Passit
2082 m

apartment buildings set around the southern portal of the tunnel. The area immediately next to the tunnel entrance consists of fenced-off grey-walled police facilities, lit by flood-lights and slightly reminiscent of control points on the former Iron Curtain.

An almost exclusively modern settlement, San Bernardino caters for walkers in summer and skiers in winter. The two-stage cableway, which starts next to the tunnel mouth, takes skiers up to **Alp de Confin**, where there are plenty of facilities for them (it only operates during winter months). In the village centre is a tourist office, a number of hotels and cafés, and a curiously unlovely octagonal church. Buses leave from next to the post office.

The village, tunnel and pass are all named after a fourteenth-century preacher who lived here-abouts. The pass was formerly called the *Passo Uccello*, meaning 'Bird Pass' and named after a near-by mountain, the Piz Uccello. The tunnel is 4 miles (6.6km) long and was opened in 1967, providing a fast through-route between Bellinzona and **Chur**, a major mountain town and rail head in eastern Switzerland. The route forms one of the fastest and most direct routes between southern Germany and northern Italy. The River Rhein, in its very early stages, occupies the valley into which the tunnel emerges at its northern end.

Passo del San Bernardino

The road over the top of the Passo del San Bernardino is not cleared of snow during the winter and is only open from around May to November. Between June and September there's a limited bus service over the pass road.

There's not actually that much to see at the top (6,775ft/2,065m): usually what there is there is a combination of low cloud, wandering cattle, and worn-out cyclists taking a breather at the café-restaurant by the road. This place (which confusingly calls itself a hospice, although it doesn't provide accommodation) sells a limited variety of meat and salad dishes, plus cuddly-toy St Bernard dogs, which famously carry a barrel of reviving brandy around their necks to re-invigorate travellers lost in the mountains. It takes about ninety minutes to walk down from the hospice to San Bernardino village, along a marked path which doesn't follow the road.

Val Calanca

The Val Calanca is a peaceful side valley to the Mesolcina. Apart from the picturesque villages along its length, and the enormously high road-bridge over the Calanca river half-way along the valley, there's nothing really specific to aim for. There are aerial cableways at **Arvigo** and **Selma**, both situated at the southern end of the valley, and numerous opportunities for walking. Rossa to Soazza over the Pass di Boffalora is a good example – allow five to six hours for this strenuous walk (use the map mentioned in the walking box opposite). Buses operate between Grono, on the main Bellinzona-Mesocco-San Bernardino route, and Rossa, which is at the head of the valley.

• SELECTED WALK •

SAN BERNARDINO VILLAGE TO ROSSA OVER THE PASS DI PASSIT

Map: San Bernardino, 267T 1:50,000

This is quite a strenuous and demanding walk which takes about five hours.

The walk begins at the lower station of the aerial cableway, just next to the entrance to the San Bernardino road tunnel (just above the station you'll see a track marker post which points the way to the Pass di Passit and Rossa). During the first ninety minutes of the walk, the path ascends through coniferous forest, fording a mountain torrent, then opens out into bleak, rocky countryside around the summit of the Pass di Passit.

From then on it's a lengthy, sometimes tricky, descent along the path which follows the Val di Passit. Some scrambling across scree and down steep banks is necessary, as is the fording of a couple of mountain rivers. The scenery, however, is spectacular with the river occupying a steep, precipitous gorge, and with numerous waterfalls cascading down the valley sides.

Around two hours from the summit of the pass, the path eventually reaches two bridges, the second of which is over the **Calancasca**, whose valley the path follows for the rest of the way. Soon after this bridge the path joins a motorised road, which leads through the picturesque hamlet of **Valbella** and then on to **Rossa**, the road situated high above another spectacular gorge. Rossa is not a particularly attractive place, but there's a hotel/café here (the Valbella) and buses leave from just over the bridge by the hotel to **Grono**, from where there are plenty of buses back to Bellinzona.

Additional Information overleaf...

PLACES TO VISIT

Bellinzona

Castelgrande
Open: daily except Monday, 10am-6pm; closed January.

Castello di Montebello
Open: as for Castelgrande.

Villa dei Cedri
Open: April-mid November, 10am-noon, 2-6pm, closed Monday; no lunchtime closing on Sunday; mid November-March, 10am-noon, 2-5pm, closed Monday.

Mesocco

Castello di Mesocco

ACCOMMODATION

Bellinzona

*** Benjaminn-Movenpick
Monte Carasso
☎ (091) 857 0171,
Fax (091) 857 7635
Part of the Movenpick hotel chain, on the Bellinzona-Locarno road in the suburb of Monte Carasso.

Castello di Montebello, Bellinzona

Hotel Gamper
Viale Stazione 29a
☎ (091) 825 3792,
Fax (091) 826 4689

*** Internazionale
Viale Stazione 29
☎ (091) 825 4333,
Fax (091) 826 1359
Best appointed hotel in Bellinzona; located opposite the station.

* San Giovanni
Via San Giovanni 7
☎/Fax (091) 825 1919
Cheaper, plainer hotel 5 minutes from the station on foot.

PUBLIC TRANSPORT

Bellinzona-Mesocco (Via Grono): 5-7 buses per day (30min).
Bellinzona-San Bernardino (Via Mesocco): 5-7 buses per day (50min).
Grono-Rossa: 5 buses per day (40min).
Bellinzona-Airolo: 1 or 2 trains or buses per hour (50min by train, 80min by bus).
Bellinzona-Locarno: 2 trains per hour (20min).
Bellinzona-Lugano: 1-2 trains per hour (25min). Other trains to Zurich and Milan.

TOURIST OFFICE

Bellinzona ☎ (091) 825 2131

The lake front at Ascona

On a map, Lake Maggiore looks like a huge blue finger poking down from the Alps into the North Italian plains. It's over 37 miles (60km) in length, yet rarely wider than 3 miles (5km), its characteristic shape a result of massive scouring by successive glaciers which pushed south from the Alps down into what is now Italy. Now it's an area of sophisticated tourism amidst lush Mediterranean climate and atmosphere.

The area is a particular favourite of rich north Europeans, who crowd out its hundreds of hotels during the summer months, soaking up the ambience of balmy weather, lush mountain scenery, elegant boutiques and lakeside promenades shaded by palm trees. The most well-healed zoom across Maggiore in swish power boats which weave in between the numerous tourist craft, windsurfers and sailing boats, their wake the only disturbance on the usually placid waters of the lake.

Around four-fifths of the lake lies within Italian territory, which includes resorts such as Stresa and Baveno, where Queen Victoria once stayed. The largest resort on the lake is Locarno, firmly in Switzerland, and the surrounding northern shores boast the most beautiful scenery of any part of the lake.

Locarno is a sophisticated, wealthy resort, and is linked by rail to the rest of Switzerland via a branch line to Bellinzona. There are chic shops, a number of worthwhile sights, and a varied and rich cultural life, which reaches a climax at the annual film festival held every August – which is one of the biggest and most highly regarded events of its kind in the world.

A cable car starts just above the town centre and rises to **Cimetta**, a high terrace spectacularly situated above the lake, giving access to some excellent walking country. **Ascona**, Locarno's westerly extension, boasts the nicest lakeside promenade and beaches.

Locarno is an ideal base from which to make excursions into the surrounding area. The three scenic valleys west and north of the city are covered in the next chapter, whilst excursions south along the eastern shore of the lake, to the Italian towns of **Luino** and **Laveno**, are covered after the description of Locarno itself.

(cont'd on page 68)

64

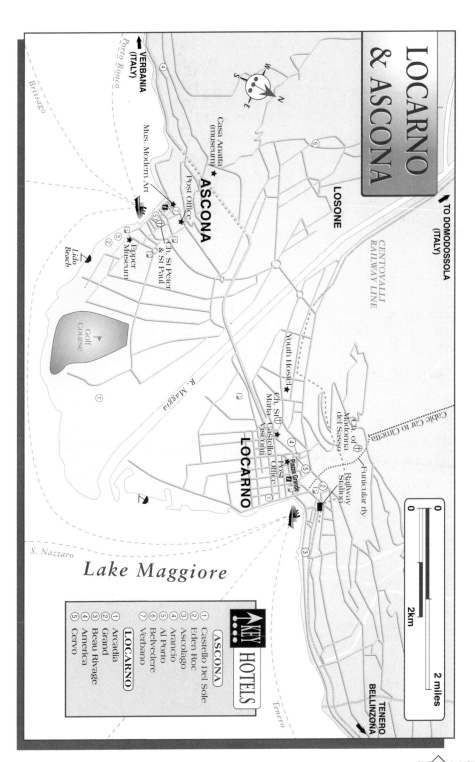

LOCARNO & ASCONA

TO DOMODOSSOLA
(ITALY)

VERBANIA
(ITALY)

Porto Ronco

Brissago

Casa Anatta
(museum)

Mus. Modern Art

Post Office

ASCONA

Ch. St Peter
& St Paul

Epper Museum

Lido Beach

Golf Course

R. Maggia

LOSONE

CENTOVALLI
RAILWAY LINE

Youth Hostel

Ch. St
Maria

Castello
Visconti

Post Office

Piazza Grande

Ch. of
Madonna
del Sasso

Funicular rly

Railway Station

Cable Car to Cimetta

LOCARNO

TENERO
BELLINZONA

S. Nazzaro

Tenero

Lake Maggiore

0   2km

0   2 miles

Above: Ascona
Below: Caffè sul lungolago, Ascona

Right: Lake front at Locarno

Below: The beach at Ascona

LOCARNO AND ASCONA

Locarno is not really a resort where people come to sight-see; they come to relax, take a stroll and sit quietly by the lake. Consequently, outside of the various summer festivals, the place will possibly be a little dull for some, but the pretty resort of Ascona is a mere bus ride away, and there are several attractive options involving travelling by cable car to **Cimetta**, above Locarno, or by boat to the botanical gardens on the **Isole di Brissago**, just down the coast from Ascona.

Locarno

Locarno's main square **Piazza Grande** isn't so much a square as a long curving boulevard. This is the main artery of the town and hosts a very useful tourist office. The Piazza Grande eventually comes to an end by a busy traffic intersection next to which is the **Castello Visconti** which used to belong to the Visconti dukes of Milan. It was built in the fourteenth century but pretty much ruined in 1518. Today it houses the town's history collection with some impressive finds from excavations of local Roman sites.

A short walk away on Via Vallemaggia is a large cemetery, one famous resident of which was Hans Arp (1887-1966). The cemetery also contains the ruins of the **church of St Maria** – only the choir remains, featuring some valuable fifteenth century wall paintings. The town's main church is the **Pilgrimage Church of the Madonna del Sasso** (founded in 1480, though substantially rebuilt in 1616),

which is situated at the top of a funicular railway (bottom station on Via Ramogna). Highlight of the interior, undoubtedly, is a superb *Flight into Egypt* by Bramantino (1536), though the reason most people trek up here is the predictably magnificent views down over Locarno and the lake. From the funicular's top station it is a short walk to the chairlift up to Cimetta di Cardada.

Above Locarno – walks and cable cars

From the Madonna del Sasso church in Locarno there's a popular cable car ride to **Cardada** (4,370ft/1,332m) and then to **Cimetta** (5,482ft/1,671m), from where there's a magnificent view over Lake Maggiore. From Cimetta it's possible to walk for around forty minutes on well-made but rocky paths up to the pointed, exposed summit of the peak **Cima della Trosa** (6,132ft/1,869m), which gives the best views in this part of the Ticino. There's a logbook kept in a watertight metal box at the summit in which walkers can sign their names. Paths run on from here to Mergoscia in the Val Verzasca (around 3hrs), from where there are buses back to Locarno. There are also paths from Cardada and Cimetta back down to Locarno, running through woodlands and hillsides strewn with villas.

THE LOCARNO FILM FESTIVAL

Every year, during the first two weeks of August, Locarno becomes something of a Mecca for film buffs. If a 9am showing of Erick Zonca's latest humanist masterpiece is your idea of a good time then this is certainly the place for you – he'll probably turn up to introduce the thing as well.

Locarno is certainly one of the world's most diverse film festivals with everything from the latest Hollywood blockbusters to short video films from emerging talents around the world. Above all, of course, it's a market-place of films looking for Europe-wide distribution, but it's a small festival in comparison with Cannes, Venice or Berlin and very much mindful of the ordinary cinema-goer – for instance, there's usually an extensive retrospective tribute to a contemporary film director.

Even for the more casual cinema-goer an evening showing in the Piazza is highly recommended. Every evening during the festival two films are shown here on an enormous 26m x 14m screen to a usually packed audience of anything up to 7,500. It's an unforgettable experience – certainly one of the most picturesque settings you'll ever see a film in.

Tickets are available from the blue ticket booths dotted around town, these also sell passes for those intent on some intense cinema-going. Ordinary tickets for the showings at the various cinemas around town are available from the venues themselves, but be warned that the tickets are generic and not sold for individual showings so they may not guarantee entry to screenings at some of the smaller venues. The information office has maps showing the location of all the cinemas and free booklets detailing all showings – look out for either *'v.o. anglaise'* or *'s-t angl'* for performances either in, or subtitled in, English. An official brochure is available for a relatively hefty outlay. For details in advance of special offers and package deals write to Ente Turistico Lago Maggiore, Incoming Services, Casa Serodine, CH-6612 Ascona.

0   **5 miles**

0   **5km**

BIGNASCO

Cima della Trosa   Cimetta

SONOGNO

Cardada

CENTOVALLI

ASCONA   LOCARNO   BELLINZONA

Magadino

Ronco   Vira

Fosano

DOMODOSSOLA

Isole di Brissago

San Nazzaro

Brissago   Gerra

Ranzo   Sant' Abbondio

Monte Tamaro

Indemini

KEY

.... Cable Car

- - - - - Boat Routes

--------- Car Ferry

Cannóbio

Maccagno

Monte Lema

N

W   E

S

Cànnero

ITALY

Lake Maggiore

LUINO

LUGANO

Ghiffa   Porto

Ponte Tresa

**LOCARNO &
LAKE MAGGIORE**

VERBANIA

Cable car
Sasso del Ferro

Laveno

**Passenger boat
on Lake Maggiore**

Ponte Brolla, Locarno

The huge cinema screen erected in the main square in Locarno for the International Film Festival

Ascona

Local bus #31 from outside the railway station takes you from the centre of Locarno across to the small, but very popular, resort of Ascona. A leisurely lakeside promenade plays host to numerous cafés, bars and restaurants. Boats frequently depart from here to all destinations around the lake.

Ascona's artistic links

Ascona has had for many years a slightly bohemian edge, playing host to a flourishing artists' community. Lenin, Jung, Hesse, Kandinsky, Klee and even Isadora Duncan have all passed through here at one time or another – consequently there are a number of small art galleries and museums in the town. Pick of the bunch is the **Museum of Modern Art** on Via Borgo which features work by Marianne von Werefkin, Richard Seewald, Franz Marc, Maurice Utrillo, Paul Klee, Hermann Hesse and Fritz Pauli. Also recommended is the **Epper Museum** on Via Albarelle which is dedicated to the work of the Swiss Expressionists Ignaz and Mischa Epper.

Other highlights of the town are the remarkable Renaissance courtyard of the Collegio Pontificio Papio (circa 1584), and the adjoining fifteenth century **church of SS Peter and Paul**. A little further afield, up Monte Verità, is a museum (the Casa Anatta) dedicated to a slightly eccentric (for the time) community of vegetarian Utopians who settled in Ascona before World War I – a 'must' stop for all hippies!

Walking south from the lakeside promenade for fifteen minutes, along a lane which runs past the backs of luxurious lakeside hotels and private villas brings one to the **lido** (entry free) – an area of sandy beach shaded by palm trees and fringed by an outdoor café and small children's water park.

Isole di Brissago

The darlings of picture postcard photographers, the **Brissago Islands** are predictably one of the most popular half-day trips from Locarno-Ascona. The particularly mild climate around here allows plants from sub-tropical regions to be grown and the larger of the islands has been turned into a botanical garden. There are specimens of sub-tropical plants from all round the world, from Texan cacti to Chinese bamboo, all crammed into a shady area of eclectic foliage which is cooled by summer breezes from the lake.

Though officially opened to the public in 1950 it seems that the islands have invited visitors for quite a while longer – Roman relics have been found here and the smaller of the two islands (which may not be visited) even has the ruins of a thirteenth century church. A restaurant in the gardens can provide a meal or refreshment, though reservations are required for evening diners.

ALONG THE EASTERN SHORE OF LAKE MAGGIORE INTO ITALY

Trains run along the eastern shore of the lake from Bellinzona, via **Vira**, across the border to **Luino**, from where there are bus and train connections to **Laveno** (and beyond to Varese, and thence Milan). There are also boat connections from Locarno to these places, and Luino is accessible by bus from Ponte Tresa on Lake Lugano, on the end of a rail line from Lugano. Undoubtedly the main attraction along the eastern shore is the Wednesday market in Luino, but travelling anywhere in the area gives a glimpse of life along the lake beyond the honey pot of Locarno/Ascona.

Around Vira and Indemini

The lakeside resorts opposite Locarno are nothing special; villas, hotels and houses compete for space with the railway and road, occupying a narrow ledge of rising land along the lake shore. **Magadino, Vira, San Nazzaro, Gerra** and **Sant' Abbondio** form a more or less continuous line of development along the lake shore. All are accessible by boat from Locarno, and by infrequent trains from Bellinzona, but it's difficult to see the attraction of visiting or staying in any of these places.

From Vira a road runs up to the hamlet of **Fosano**, a very peaceful spot with an inexpensive outdoor terrace restaurant which has a fabulous view over the lake. Beyond Fosano the road runs up a series of corkscrew twists, ascending through forests and eventually out into open countryside as it crosses a low pass (4,577ft/1,395m). A path from here runs up to the summit of Monte Tamaro (see page 114). The road then descends towards **Indemini**. The village lies at the head of the Giona valley, most of which is in Italy; there's a border post just beyond Indemini, and the road continues down the picturesque valley through more villages to reach the Italian shore of the lake at Maccagno. Although Indemini is pretty, with a couple of restaurants and views over the steeply forested valley, there's nothing specific to see here.

Luino

The major town on the eastern shore of Maggiore, **Luino**, is remarkable chiefly for its Wednesday market when the town's streets become claustrophobically crammed with stalls selling everything from lemons and limes to liquor and laundry mats. It's quite a busy little town but there's little to do except take in the views across the lake. Piazza Garibaldi, the main square, features the first ever statue erected in honour of Garibaldi in Italy – it was here that he raised a small army to fight the Austrians after defeat at the Battle of Custozza.

Luino is reputed to be the birthplace of painter Bernadino Luini, and the church of San Pietro in the eastern part of town features an *Adoration of the Magi* thought to be by his hand. For anyone really desperate for something to do, there's also a small town museum on Palazzo Verbania.

Laveno

A quarter of an hour by regular train from Luino is **Laveno**, which boasts a breathtaking cable car ride up Sasso del Ferro (3,485ft/1,062m). The journey up is in an orange bin fit for two people which is totally exposed to the elements, but the view from the top across the lake to Monte Rosa is truly awesome – the panorama over the Italian plain seems to just go on forever. The walk from the top station up to the summit takes about thirty minutes but the views are not significantly better.

Left: Locarno

Below: Isole di Brissago

Below: The lake front at Ascona

Visitors to Laveno, on the Italian shore of Maggiore, can ascend the mountain above the town by cable car

PLACES TO VISIT

Locarno

Museum, open daily except Monday, 10am-5pm.

Ascona

Epper Museum
Open: April, May, June, September, October, 10am-noon, 3-6pm, Tues-Fri only; July, August, 10am-noon, 8-10pm, Tues-Fri, and 8-10pm only weekends.

Modern Art Museum
Open: March-December 10am-noon, 3-6pm, Tuesday-Saturday; 10am-noon only on Sunday.

ACCOMMODATION

For a complete list of the dozens of accommodation possibilities in Ascona and Locarno ask for the brochure *Lago Maggiore: Ascona, Locarno, Brissago; hotels*, published every year. Those listed below form merely a selection.

Ascona

***** **Castello del Sole**
Via Muraccio 142
☎ (091) 791 0202,
Fax (091) 792 1118
e-mail:castellosole@bluewin.ch
Luxurious hotel with fitness centre, swimming pool, private beach, golf, tennis, restaurants.

**** **Ascolago**
Via Albarelle
☎ (091) 791 2055,
Fax (091) 791 4226
Lakeside location; sailing and motorboats; extensive watersports; lakeside terrace restaurant.

*** **Al Porto**
Piazza G. Motta
☎ (091) 785 8585,
Fax (091) 785 8586
Rooms set around a small courtyard in the heart of Ascona.

** **Arancio**
Via Collinetta 78
☎ (091) 791 2333,
Fax (091) 791 5802
Family-run hotel on the corniche between Ascona and Brissago; swimming pool, views over the lake.

* **Belvedere**
Via Locarno 19
☎ (091) 791 4222
Small hotel on Ascona-Locarno road; short walk from the shops and lake shore.

Verbano
Via Borgo 19
☎ (091) 791 1274
One of the cheapest hotels in Ascona; no showers in the rooms. Short distances from Ascona centre and the lake.

Locarno

**** Arcadia al Lago
Via Orelli 5
☎ (091) 756 1818,
Fax (091) 756 1828
Family-oriented hotel on the
lakeside promenade; big
apartments with balconies.

**** Grand Hotel
Via Sempione 17
☎ (091) 743 0282,
Fax (091) 743 3013
Classic hotel with large
garden and swimming pool,
close to the lake and town
centre.

*** Beau Rivage
Viale Verbano 31
☎ (091) 743 1355,
Fax (091) 743 9409
Elegant hotel three minutes
walk from central Locarno,
on the lakeside promenade.

** America
Piazza Grande
☎ (091) 751 7635,
Fax (091) 752 3616
Situated in the heart of Locarno.

* Cervo
Via Torretta 11
☎ (091) 751 4131
Small hotel in the heart of
Locarno; less expensive
than other city centre hotels.

Bellavista
Via B. Varenna 31
☎ (091) 751 2431,
Fax (091) 752 3684
Small hotel five minutes from
Locarno centre on foot.

Ostello Palagiovani
Via B. Varenna 18
☎ (091) 756 1500,
Fax (091) 756 1501
e-mail: info@youthhostel.ch
http://www.youthhostel.ch
Fifteen minute walk from Locarno
centre; bus 31/36; Member of
Swiss Youth Hostels Association;
dormitories.

PUBLIC TRANSPORT

Locarno is linked to Bellinzona by two trains per hour (25min) and two
buses per hour (50min). There is one train every two hours on the
Bellinzona-Vira-Luino route.

TOURIST INFORMATION

Locarno

Via Luini 3, ☎ (091) 791 0091, Fax (091) 785 1941
e-mail: buongiorno@maggiore.ch

*S*ome of the highest and most scenic areas of the Ticino are to be found in the mountains to the west and north of Locarno. The three main valleys – the Centovalli, which runs west into Italy, and the Maggia and Verzasca, which are both 'dead end' valleys running north from the lake into the heart of the Ticino Alps – are very popular day excursions from Locarno due to their proximity to the lakeside resort.

Of the three valleys, Verzasca is the shortest and most popular, with opportunities for bathing, bungy jumping (off the Verzasca Dam), sightseeing and gentle walking. The Centovalli offers opportunities for excursions on foot, by train and by cable car; and the Maggia, the longest valley, gives access to the most stunning mountain scenery, around Robiei, reached by Ticino's most spectacular cable car ride.

This valley also has the area's only skiing facilities, situated above the German-speaking enclave of Bosco Gurin, which is the highest village in The Ticino.

Throughout the area there are numerous picturesque villages, most notably **Lavertezzo** (Verzasca), **Fusio** and the hamlets on the road to San Carlo (Maggia), Bosco Gurin (Maggia), and Intragna and Rasa (Centovalli).

THE CENTOVALLI

The Val Centovalli – 'valley of a hundred valleys' – is one of the most attractive areas of Switzerland. Situated to the west of Locarno, it's essentially the course of the River Melezza, which has cut a magnificently narrow, deep steep-sided gorge into the mountains, which in turn is dissected by numerous tributaries and other small streams – the 'hundred valleys'. Settlements nestle in the shady valley bottom or cling to sunny, cooler ledges

Viaduct on the Centovalli rail line at Intragna

along its sides, which are peppered with small farms surrounded by woods and upland pastures. There are many opportunities for walkers here; others will be happy just touring the valley by road, train and aerial cableway, although it should be remembered that the valley is justifiably popular and can get busy.

The Centovalli Rail Line

The most scenic rail line in the Ticino runs along this valley, from an underground terminus in Locarno adjacent to the mainline rail station, across the Italian border at Camedo to Domodossola, on the main Milan-Brig-Geneva rail route. It's a metre gauge line, the narrow width between the rails allowing the line to take circuitous loops around the steep bluffs and across precipitous gorges en route.

Fast trains take just over thirty minutes to reach the border at Camedo, although they do not stop at every station; the Italian section of the journey from Camedo to Domodossola takes just over an hour. Stopping trains between Locarno and Camedo take slightly longer and do not continue into Italy. It's an excellent way to travel in the Centovalli, as services begin and terminate right in the centre of Locarno, trains are frequent and regular, and connections onto aerial cableways at Intragna and Verdasio are very easy.

Intragna

The Centovalli really begins at Intragna, an attractively situated village 5 miles/8km (or 17min by train) west of Locarno. Here the valley narrows abruptly, and the road and railway have to cross the steep gorge of the Isorno river before reaching the village, which languishes on a hillside surrounded by vineyards. The main square is just up from the station; it's an irregular space, dark and shady, where you'll find an expensive restaurant (which overlooks the valley) and the village church, whose 230ft (70m) high tower is one of the tallest in The Ticino. If it's open you can take a quick look at the interior, with its stucco galleries and rococo embellishments.

Costa

Down by the railway and road bridges is the lower station of an aerial cableway up to Costa, which is less appealing than Intragna. The two settlements are linked by a marked path (45min downhill; 90min uphill). There isn't really that much to see or do at Costa, and with the walking opportunities and scenery better further west, most people will want to press on along the valley.

Verdasio

The road and railway line stick to the north side of the valley past Intragna, curving and crossing one another at intervals. At **Corcapolo**, spread out along the road and rail tracks, there are a couple of roadside bars. The next point of interest is **Verdasio** (seven minutes by train beyond Intragna), where the railway line curves into the valley side to cross yet another splashing gulley on an arched viaduct. Adjacent to the roadside and station is the lower terminus of an aerial cableway which is slung right across the valley, taking a single suspended cabin at a time up to Rasa.

Rasa & Monti di Comino

There is no road access to Rasa – the people here are solely dependent on the cableway or farm vehicles using mountain tracks. Situated on a high, cool ledge, Rasa is a cluster of stone-clad houses and farm buildings set either side of a long, winding lane. There's a small restaurant and a magnificent panorama up and down the valley (follow the signs to reach the best viewpoint).

Rasa is easily the best starting point for walks in the Centovalli. The easiest and shortest option is to walk back down to Corcapolo station (90min) or Intragna (2hrs), through woods and farms and finally along and across the river, bubbling along in its gorge. More adventurous walkers will want to head over the Alpe di Naccio Pass and then down to Brissago on Lake Maggiore, from where there are buses and boats back to Ascona and Locarno. This second option takes four to five hours and is steep in places.

Just along the road from Verdasio station is the lower station of another cableway up to Monti di Comino (3,280ft/ 1,000m), from where walking opportunities are rather more limited, and the view is rather less spectacular.

Beyond Verdasio

Road and railway continue to cling to the valley side beyond Verdasio. **Palagnedra**, an attractive village on the south facing slopes of the valley, is reached by a road turning off to the left, a short distance beyond Verdasio. The **church of San Michele** in the village boasts vivid fifteenth century frescoes.

The road to Palagnedra crosses the valley by means of a dam that supports the lake occupying the remainder of the valley as far as **Camedo** and the Swiss frontier post. Immediately beyond the station at Camedo the road and railway cross over a bridge to the Italian frontier post at Ponte Ribellasca.

The Italians know their part of the line as *La Vigezzina* and the valley it runs through as the *Vigezzo*. The train passes through a dozen tiny villages between Ribellasca and Domodossola, each with its own immaculately kept tiny church and colourful station, strewn with flowerbeds. Most stations have a red-and-white signal on the platform which must be raised to get trains to stop.

Domodossola itself, reached after the train has made a steep descent into the broad valley of the Toce river by several loops, has an attractive medieval centre, with an arcaded, ancient square. It's a major rail hub: from here, trains run north through the Simplon tunnel to Brig, Geneva, central Switzerland and on into Germany and France, and south to Milan and central Italy.

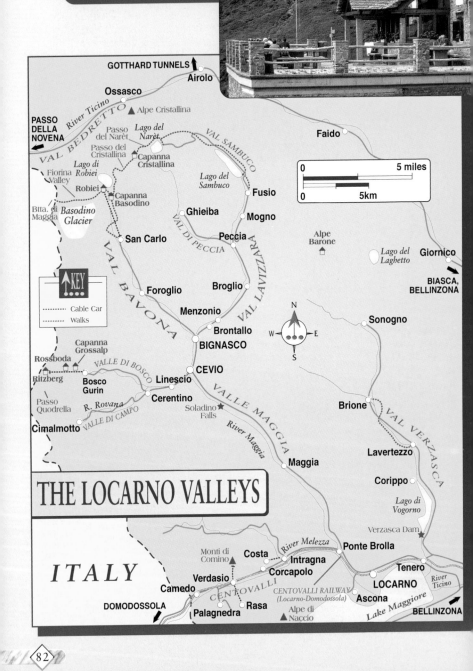

The Capanna Basodino near Robiei

GOTTHARD TUNNELS

Airolo

Ossasco

River Ticino

PASSO DELLA NOVENA

VAL BEDRETTO

▲ Alpe Cristallina

Faido

Passo del Narèt

Lago del Narèt

VAL SAMBUCO

Passo del Cristallina

Capanna Cristallina

Fiorina Valley

Lago di Robiei

Lago del Sambuco

Robiei

Fusio

Capanna Basodino

Ghieiba

Mogno

Btta. di Maggia

Basodino Glacier

VAL DI PECCIA

Peccia

Alpe Barone

Lago del Laghetto

Giornico

San Carlo

VAL LAVIZZARA

BIASCA, BELLINZONA

VAL BAVONA

Foroglio

Broglio

KEY

········· Cable Car

········· Walks

Menzonio

Brontallo

BIGNASCO

Sonogno

Capanna Grossalp

N

Rossboda

VALLE DI BOSCO

CEVIO

W   E

Ritzberg

Bosco Gurin

Linescio

S

Passo Quodrella

Cerentino

R. Rovana

VALLE DI CAMPO

Soladino Falls ★

VALLE MAGGIA

Brione

VAL VERZASCA

Cimalmotto

River Maggia

Lavertezzo

Maggia

Corippo

Lago di Vogorno

THE LOCARNO VALLEYS

Verzasca Dam ★

River Melezza

Ponte Brolla

Monti di Comino ▲

Costa

Intragna

Tenero

ITALY

Verdasio

Corcapolo

LOCARNO

River Ticino

Camedo

CENTOVALLI

CENTOVALLI RAILWAY (Locarno-Domodossola)

Ascona

Lake Maggiore

DOMODOSSOLA

Palagnedra

Rasa

Alpe di Naccio ▲

BELLINZONA

0 —————— 5 miles
0 —————— 5km

82

Bosco Gurin, highest village in the Ticino

Around Robiei, accessible by cable car from San Carlo at the head of the Val Bavona

THE VALLE MAGGIA

The Valle Maggia, running north from Ponte Brolla, just west of Locarno, is the least visited of the three valleys, partly because its attractions are rather far-flung. Bosco-Gurin, San Carlo (with its spectacular cable car journey to Robiei) and Fusio, which all lie at the head of the three different valleys into which the Valle Maggia separates beyond Cevio, are well over an hour's journey by road from Locarno. Nonetheless, this is where the most spectacular scenery of the Locarno valleys is, particularly around Robiei, one of the best walking bases in The Ticino. Bosco Gurin is the area's only skiing base, and it too is good for walks.

Locarno to Cevio & Bignasco

The valley begins at **Ponte Brolla**, where the road crosses the Centovalli rail line on a level crossing. Many people use the stretch of the Maggia river north of here for swimming and sun bathing in summer. The road follows the river at the bottom of a typical glacial valley – a flat valley floor bounded by precipitous sides.

Shortly before reaching **Maggia** there's a church on the left, the **chapel of St Madonna delle Grazie,** which boasts a painted wooden ceiling and frescoes from the sixteenth century. A little way beyond Maggia the 300ft (91m) high **Soladino Falls** splash down the western side of the valley.

Cevio is the largest town in the valley. Situated on the left as the road enters the town is one of its most distinctive buildings – the valley hospital, a porticoed building from around the turn of the century. Cevio's main town square is set a little back from the main road, to the left; its most notable building is the Casa Pretorio, the former court house, showing the coats-of-arms of the Maggia villages and of the Landvogts, the first Swiss governors. The presence of German speakers in the valley is reflected in the inscriptions underneath some of the coats of arms. Close by is the eighteenth-century residence of the Landvogt governors. As the road runs north from Cevio it passes by the regional museum of the Maggia Valley.

Five minutes beyond Cevio is **Bignasco**, where the valley divides. Bignasco is also an attractive village, its houses set around a bridge over the river. The church plays a *carillon* chime twice a day, although it's only likely to be heard by visitors who choose to stay here.

Bignasco and Cevio are both centrally located in the Valle Maggia, and so make excellent bases from which to see the attractions described in this section.

West from Cevio – the Campo and Bosco valleys

From the post office on the main square at Cevio a bus service operates four to five times per day west along **Valle di Bosco**, whose main village is Bosco Gurin, an important walking and skiing centre. The road from Cevio ascends a number of potentially nausea-inducing corkscrew twists as it climbs 820ft (250m) to **Linescio**, in the narrow, steep-sided valley of the River Rovana.

A short distance beyond this the valley divides at **Cerentino**, with a turning heading up through the village along the **Valle di Campo** to **Cimalmotto**. A very limited post bus service operates along this isolated valley, between Cerentino and Cimalmotto, but most visitors will carry on along the main road from Cerentino to the head of the Valle di Bosco at Bosco Gurin, reached after fifty minutes by bus from Cevio.

Bosco Gurin

Bosco Gurin (4,930ft/1,503m), where the road terminates, is the highest permanently inhabited village in the Ticino. The road ends outside the post office, where there's a car park and two restaurants. Beyond this, stone and wood buildings cluster along steep, narrow car-less lanes, lending the village an air of timelessness and remoteness.

The church, surrounded by an immaculately attended graveyard, is the centre of the village, and is a surprisingly large and robust building for such a small community. Beyond it and just below it, the village museum (the Walserhaus) gives visitors an insight into the life and history of one of the region's most isolated communities. It's housed in a former dwelling, a typical wooden building, and although all the wording of the exhibits is in German and Italian, it's worth looking around just to gauge the sort of life led by villagers in these parts in the past. In particular, the museum celebrates the unique language characteristics of the area.

In truth, Bosco Gurin has suffered greatly from depopulation during the twentieth century, which is why its economic base

(cont'd on page 88)

• WALKS FROM BOSCO GURIN •

Bosco Gurin is an excellent walking centre – here are a few suggestions for some easy-to-moderate rated walks. From **Capanna Grossalp**, close to the chairlift station at Rossboda, it's an easy fifty-minute walk back down to Bosco Gurin, or, it's a walk of one hour thirty minutes to the summit of the **Passo Quadrella**, situated at 7,011ft (2,137m). From here the path continues down to the hamlet of Cimalmotto, at the head of the Valle di Campo, and is reached after a further one hour and thirty minutes. From here there's a limited bus service to Cerentino, on the Cevio-Bosco Gurin bus route; alternatively there's a marked path from Cimalmotto to Cerentino, although much of it runs along the road. The Italian border lies a short distance up from Grossalp, and it can be crossed via the **Gurinerfurka Pass** on the more challenging route from Grossalp to Fondovalle (Italy).

Around Robiei, accessible by cable car from San Carlo at the head of the Val Bavona

The German speakers of Bosco Gurin

A glance at a map of the upper area of the Valle di Bosco shows some place names which don't seem immediately at home in Italian-speaking Ticino: Grossalp, Ritzberg, Grosshorn, Andatschei and Wolfstaffel all indicate the fact that the area around Bosco Gurin is a German-speaking enclave, which is unique in this part of Switzerland. The uniqueness of the linguistic inheritance has the same roots as the reasons for the settlement's remoteness.

Back in the early thirteenth century the area around Bosco was in the hands of Lombardian (ie north Italian) landowners. They needed tough soldiers for their military campaigns and selected farmers from the region of the upper Valais (Wallis), a region of very high mountains (and consequently hard farming conditions) around 25 miles (40km) due north of Bosco.

When their military campaigning was done, the Wallisians were offered land in return for their services; but they spoke German, and wouldn't be accepted in any of the villages held by their Lombardian landlords, which were all Italian speaking. So an area of previously unoccupied land was chosen for them, in the remote upper reaches of the Valle di Bosco. Here they began a new community and the area has been German-speaking ever since.

Over the years the language spoken in the valley has evolved into a unique dialect of German with many Italian influences. Although Bosco Gurin only has around sixty inhabitants, there have been great efforts made to preserve this unique way of speaking.

Around the village Gothic script is used for the names of houses and on grave inscriptions – this is common practice in Bavaria and German-speaking Switzerland, but is otherwise unheard of in the Ticino. Many of the names on the headstones around the church are a strange mixture of Italian and German. The fact that the current owners of the town's supermarket share the same surname as those on the graves indicates a long continuity of inhabitancy of the village by a relatively small number of families.

has been widened to make it a fairly important centre for skiing. Facilities include ski tows in the area immediately beyond the village, and a two-stage chairlift (opened in 1998 and not marked on older maps). The chairlift runs from below the village up to **Rossboda** and then to a final station situated at 7,875ft (2,400m) on the slopes below the summit of **Ritzberg**, the peak which glowers over the village. The first stage of the chairlift usually works in summer, giving access to some good walking countryside. A five-minute walk down from Rossboda station is a mountain hut, **Capanna Grossalp**, situated amidst deserted, stone-built agricultural buildings with an excellent view down the valley.

North-west from Bignasco – the Val Bavona & Robiei

A bus service operates five times per day (decreasing to twice a day in Winter) from the post office at Bignasco along the beautiful **Val Bavona** to the village of San Carlo. The villages the road passes through on this twenty-five minute journey are typical of the upper Ticino – houses are built and covered entirely in stone and some of the villagers still work on the surrounding land in addition to keeping poultry and tending small allotments in plots close to their homes.

As in other areas of upland Ticino, the area has suffered out-migration, and tourism is now the mainstay of the economy. Restaurants and *grotti* line the road to San Carlo, and at **Foroglio** there's a restaurant next to a magnificent waterfall, which tumbles down the valley side.

San Carlo, at the head of the valley, is slightly larger and less instantly appealing than the other villages. The bus terminates here or, when the cable car is in operation, next to the lower station, 550yd (500m) on from the centre of the village.

The cable car to Robiei is the focus of the Valle Maggia for most visitors. The enormous cars, capable of holding over one hundred people (in a tight squeeze), dangle over the precipitous slopes of the upper Val Bavona as they rise nearly 3,280ft (1,000m) from San Carlo to Robiei, a sunny plateau surrounded by some of the most spectacular scenery in The Ticino. On a clear day, the view across to the ice flows of the **Basodino Glacier**, which lies hard up against the Italian border, are stunning.

The octagonal building above the cable car station is a restaurant and hotel (separate rooms and dormitories; see end of chapter for details) and the whole place is overlooked to the east by a dam which holds in the **Lago di Robiei**. Another lift runs from Robiei to a further height of over 8,202ft (2,500m), but it's for works use only, associated with the underground hydroelectric power station and the linked series of artificial and natural lakes in this part of the mountains. Many people are satisfied with the view from the terrace outside the restaurant at Robiei, but for those who aren't, this is the starting point for a number of hikes, some of which are difficult but run through spectacular scenery.

• WALKS FROM ROBIEI •

There is a huge number of possibilities as regards walks from Robiei. Paths lead from here across to Airolo and All'Acqua, in the north-western Ticino (Chapter One), taking around six to seven hours, with a long journey back to Locarno or the Valle Maggia on public transport.

There are a number of *capanna* in the mountains (some of which are unmanned) around which hikes lasting more than a day can be planned. The hotel/hostel at Robiei, and the Capanna Basodino, five minutes away down the hill from the top cable car station, also offer accommodation (see end of chapter for details).

The following three walks below are suggestions which vary in difficulty and length.

1 THE FIORINA VALLEY

This beautiful secluded valley runs west from Robiei up towards **Bocchetta di Vallemaggia**, a high pass (8,645ft/ 2,635m) on the border with Italy. The path from Robiei to the pass takes around two hours thirty minutes to walk and is difficult in the upper stages. In fact, many walkers will end up turning back before they get to the summit of the pass, defeated by the weather closing in, the large amounts of snow on the ground (even in August) or the difficult rock-hopping which the path entails.

Things are fairly straightforward as far as **Randinascia** (40min from Robiei), a beautiful area of high, rocky, marshy meadowland where there's an old farm building and a basic shelter made from rocks, piled up, to enclose the space left under a huge overhanging boulder. Things begin to get tricky though as the path curves round to the right to ascend the pass, with lots of rock-hopping across piles of huge, jagged boulders. The views across to the glacier (the path runs close to it but doesn't run up to it) are tremendous as the path climbs up from Randinascia, and the scenery throughout is spectacular.

2 ROBIEI TO SAN CARLO

This is a straightforward and popular walk down the valley above which the cable car dangles. It takes around two hours thirty minutes and is a good option if there's cloud at altitudes above Robiei.

(cont'd overleaf)

(cont'd from previous page)

From Robiei take the road for five minutes to the **Capanna Basodino**, a mountain hut where there are refreshments and accommodation available. From here the path runs downwards quite steeply, passing through the high-walled gorge of the river before entering woodland for the final stages. A notice shortly before the end of the walk advises that in times of heavy rain the path turns into a river! The path emerges on the road between San Carlo village and the cable car station. There's a good restaurant in the village, whose shady terrace is always full of worn-out hikers by late afternoon in summer.

↑3 ROBIEI TO FUSIO VIA THE CRISTALLINA AND NARÈT PASSES

This is the longest, most difficult, but also the most spectacular walk described in this book. It takes between seven and eight hours and runs from Robiei, crossing two passes, to Fusio at the head of the Val Lavizzara. Public transport timings may mean that it is impossible to complete this walk in a day. In which case accommodation may need to be found at one of the

Fusio

two hostels by the top cable car station in Robiei, at Fusio, or at the Capanna Cristallina, a mountain hut situated a third of the way into the walk, and only accessible on foot.

Stage One: Robiei to Capanna Cristallina (2-3 hours)

The first part of the walk, from Robiei to **Sfundau Lake**, can be done via a number of different routes. The quickest is to walk for forty minutes up the paved road from Robiei, to the top station of the works cable car which runs up from Robiei. The road continues on to the Cavagnoli dam, but at the cable car station take the path which runs upwards – it's easy to follow and after another forty minutes it emerges, above Sfundau Lake, into a spectacularly bleak, high and remote landscape. Keep following the path as it runs high above the southern, then eastern

(cont'd overleaf)

• WALKS FROM ROBIEI •

(cont'd from previous page)

shore of the lake, joining another path which comes in from the right (the latter is another option to get here from Robiei). The path runs along the edge of a steep precipice and there are ropes attached with metal spikes to the side of the rock to help walkers cope with this section.

From Sfundau, keep following the path as it rises and crosses the **Passo del Cristallina**. Soon after the pass is crossed **Capanna Cristallina**, a remote mountain hut set at the bottom of a shallow valley, comes into view; it takes around thirty minutes to reach it. There is accommodation available here in dormitories (see end of chapter for details) and refreshments including cooked meals. From the cabin, paths run down to Alpe Cristallina, which is a point on the Val Bedretto walk described on page 29 and then down to Ossasco, from where there are buses to Airolo.

Stage Two: Capanna Cristallina to Fusio (4-5 hours)

From the capanna, take the clearly marked path which runs downhill, crosses the river and then starts climbing the **Passo del Narèt**. Since the cabin is situated at 7,707ft (2,349m) there isn't that much in the way of vertical ascent on this pass, but the path is difficult and rocky with ropes in one place to help walkers pull themselves up the steepest parts. There's a magnificent view from here across the Val Bedretto which almost takes in the road up to the St Gotthard Pass, but this is hidden behind the jut of a mountain. From the top of the pass, forty to fifty minutes from the cabin, **Lago del Narèt** hoves into view, an artificial lake held back (unusually) behind two dams. It takes around forty minutes to follow the path around the lake and *steeply* down onto the dam itself.

There's a road to the dam from Fusio but the marked path takes its own course along the Val Sambuco, running down a steep valley below the dam to some farm buildings on the road (where the farm's own cheese and other products are on sale). From here the path runs to the right of the road, before following it for a while, and then running high above **Lago del Sambuco**, another artificial reservoir dammed for hydroelectric processes. The path runs down steeply to meet the dam after taking a fairly level course for some time. Fusio is reached around thirty minutes or so beyond the dam; there are restaurants and accommodation facilities here, and a bus service to Bignasco.

North-east from Bignasco – the Val Lavizzara to Fusio

The right-hand of the two valleys which runs north from Bignasco – the **Val Lavizzara** – is far less visited than the Val Bavona. The bus journey along the valley is particularly arduous as the bus makes several detours to remote mountain villages, such as Brontallo and Menzonio, which are situated high above the main valley. At **Peccia** a side valley (that of the River Peccia) joins the main valley. There's no public transport along it and after passing through a couple of hamlets the road stops at **Ghieiba**, from where there's a path running up steeply to the **Lago del Narèt** (see walks opposite).

After Peccia the main valley road begins to get steeper, by-passing the village of **Mogno** to the right. Here a modern church designed by noted Swiss architect Mario Botta, has the form of a giant glass leaf inverted to catch the sun. **Fusio** itself, reached after a fairly steep climb, is one of the most picturesque villages in the Locarno valleys, a jumble of houses perched on the valley side, best viewed from the outdoor terrace restaurant of the Albergo Pineta, to the right as the road enters the town.

There's no public transport beyond Fusio, but the road continues up the wild **Val Sambuco**, running past **Lago del Sambuco** and then steeply up to terminate at yet another hydro electric reservoir, **Lago del Narèt**. From here there's a path to Robiei, at the top of the San Carlo cable car (around 4-5hrs).

THE VAL VERZASCA

The most easterly of the valleys, the **Val Verzasca** runs from Tenero, just east of Locarno, north to the mountain village of Sonogno, where the bus route along the valley ends. The valley is undeniably

Verzasca Dam

Five to ten minutes from Tenero the mighty Verzasca Dam (Diga Verzasca) looms up through the trees on the left hand side. Access to the dam is from a small car park (and bus stop) on the left hand side of the road, where the local tourist office has also set up a souvenir shop and information centre for the valley.

The dam was built in the early 1960s and is awesomely high. From the road across the top there's an outstanding view straight down into the vertically-sided gorge which the river carved out of the mountainside. This is now dry – the water which flooded a large section of the lower valley is now held back in the lake.

The dam was made famous in an abseiling scene in the James Bond film *Goldeneye*. Exploiting its height and spectacular location, a local firm operates bungy jumping from the top, claiming it's one of the highest bungy jumps in the world (Trekking Team ☎ 091 780 7800).

Ponte dei Salti, Lavertezzo

attractive, with its narrow wooded sides dotted with tiny settlements and its rushing river, which is popular with swimmers and sunbathers in summer. However, the charms of the valley are very well known and on warm days it gets *very* popular, as it's a favourite excursion for visitors to Locarno.

Tenero, linked to Locarno in about five minutes by both bus and train, is really an easterly extension of that resort, and not particularly attractive. The Val Verzasca road heads up past villas, apartment blocks and vineyards, into the wooded slopes of the valley, negotiating a couple of steep bluffs by means of twisting tunnels.

Lavertezzo

The next village beyond Verzasca Dam, accessible on a side turning, is **Corippo**, whose stone houses occupy a narrow shelf of land on the opposite side of the valley. Once famous for its linen weaving, the village is a national monument, owing to its site and the state of preservation of its original character.

Five minutes beyond the turning for Corippo the road runs through **Lavertezzo**, the prettiest and most visited of the villages in the valley. Here the gushing green waters of the river churn over smooth granite rocks in raging torrents, interspersed with deep pools of comparative stillness. The river flows under the architectural highlight of the valley, the *Ponte dei Salti*, a medieval double-arched bridge. It's a remarkable site, distinctive, beautiful and popular; a number of *grotti* and restaurants cater for the swarms of visitors.

On warm days in summer many people come to this part of the

river to sun bathe and swim: notices in four different languages surround the site detailing how dangerous this is, because of the fast currents and the sloping, smooth rocks which get very slippery. Despite the warnings there are always lots of people here (and at sites further up the river), many of them with children taking advantage of the cold water and spectacular location (and even diving off the bridge). The risks are spelled out carefully and in the end it's up to individuals to decide whether or not they wish to bathe in these tempting but potentially very dangerous surroundings.

Above: The rocks at Lavertezzo make an exciting bathing area

Below: Sonogno

Brione

The next major village along the valley is Brione. Known for its

Senitiero per Arte

Lavertezzo and Brione are linked by a walking trail called the *Sentiero per l'Arte*. It's an easy walk of a little under two hours between the two settlements, on a clearly marked path along which local artists display some of their sculptures – hence the name. From Lavertezzo the path hugs the riverbank tightly and runs past more areas used for bathing. After an hour or so it crosses a bridge and runs up to the road: here walkers should head down the road for a short distance and cross the road bridge where the trail picks up again on the other side of the valley.

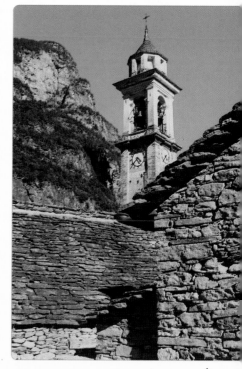

granite quarrying, it's home to the most important church in the valley, **Sta Maria Assunta**, which is located on the main square, to the left as the road passes through. The building is thirteenth century, with many later additions: there's a fresco of St Christopher on the outside, with fading medieval frescoes on the walls of the interior, which is otherwise quite plain.

Sonogno and the mountains beyond

Buses terminate at Sonogno, 4.4 miles (7km) beyond Brione, where the valley splits into two spurs. The settlement is not particularly appealing, and rather tourist-driven, with a shop selling local handicrafts, a number of restaurants and *grotti*, and a museum.

The museum is worth a visit. An information booklet in English is available to guide visitors around the exhibits which illustrate traditional life in the valley in times gone by, when activities revolved around cheese making, gathering chestnuts and preparing, each summer, for the cold winter to follow.

The paths that head into the mountains beyond Sonogno are difficult, lengthy and less well trodden than those in the other valleys involving long and fairly arduous ascents. Walks run across passes to Biasca in the main Ticino valley and to Broglio, north of Bignasco in the Valle Maggia – both take around six to seven hours to complete. In addition there are paths that run into high, inhospitable mountains to the north, around Lake Laghetto, and the mountain hut Alpe Barone.

PLACES TO VISIT

Cevio

Museo di Valmaggia
Open: April-October, 10am-noon, 2-6pm, Tues-Sat; 2-6pm, Sunday.

Sonogno

Museo di Val Verzasca
Open: May-October, daily 11.30am-4.30pm.

Bosco Gurin

Walserhaus (Museum)
Open: Easter-October, 10.15-11.30am, 1.30-5pm, Tues-Sat, 1.30-5pm Sunday.

ACCOMMODATION

Most people see the Locarno valleys from a base in Locarno. Accommodation possibilities in the valleys include:

Centovalli

** Hotel Antico
Intragna, ☎ (091) 796 1107, Fax (091) 796 3115
Small hotel in the heart of this delightful village.

Al Forno
Intragna, ☎ (091) 796 1179
No road access; reached by Intragna cable car; ideal for walkers; inexpensive hotel in beautiful countryside.

Campanile
Intragna, ☎ (091) 796 1897
Family-run pension; modern building; inexpensive.

Elvetico Hotel
Camedo, ☎ (091) 798 1095
Inexpensive hotel located on Centovalli line at the Swiss/Italian border.

Valle Maggia

Hotel Edelweiss
Bosco Gurin, ☎ (091) 754 1900,
Fax (091) 754 1946

Hotel Walser
Bosco Gurin, ☎ (091) 759 0202,
Fax (091) 759 0203

Ristorante Basodino
Cevio, ☎ (091) 754 1101,
Fax (091) 754 2252
Open summer only; restaurant
with rooms; walkers' hotel,
just below lower Robiei cable
car station.

Hotel della Posta
Bignasco, ☎ (091) 754 1123,
Fax (091) 754 2257
Inexpensive hotel in nice location,
overlooking river in Bignasco;
central position in
Valle Maggia.

Albergo Robiei
☎ (091) 756 5020,
Fax (091) 756 5025
Dormitory hostel at top of Robiei
cable car; open summer only.

Capanna Cristallina
☎ (091) 869 2330
Mountain hut; dormitory
accommodation.

Val Verzasca

*** Campofelice
Via alle Brere, Tenero
☎ (091) 735 6300,
Fax (091) 735 6363
Modern high-rise hotel
with all mod cons.

Ristorante Alpino
Sonogno
☎ (091) 746 1163
Small restaurant with
rooms in centre of village.

PUBLIC TRANSPORT

Buses

Locarno (railway station) -Tenero-Verzasca Dam-Lavertezzo-Sonogno:
roughly one bus every two hours. Service is better in the morning. Only
four buses per day on Sundays. Total journey time Locarno-Sonogno:
70min.

Locarno (railway station) **-Bignasco:** hourly service; 50min to Cevio,
55min to Bignasco.

Cevio-Bosco Gurin: 4-5 buses per day (45min).

Bignasco-San Carlo (for Robiei cable car): 2-4 buses per day (30min).

Bignasco-Fusio: 3-5 buses per day (40min).

TOURIST OFFICES

Val Verzasca
Tenero
☎ (091) 745 1661,
Fax (091) 745 4230

Valle Maggia
Maggia
☎ (091) 753 1885,
Fax (091) 753 2212

The area around Lugano and Como is the most popular in the Ticino with good reason. There's a huge amount to see and do here – from chugging across the lake in the numerous passenger ferries, to window-shopping among the chic boutiques of Lugano; from taking in some of the city's cultural life, to walking in the appealing surrounding countryside.

The region is dominated by Lake Lugano (Ceresio to locals) of which Lugano is the chief resort. The lake is a curious shape with twisting, branching arms that filled with water after being scoured out by glaciers during the most recent ice advance from the Alps. The western and eastern extremities of the lake lie in Italian territory. Compared to Lakes Como and Maggiore, it covers a comparatively small area, but it is this fact, combined with the excellent road, rail and boat connections, which makes travelling around here so enjoyable and easy.

The region can be seen from one base. Although Lugano is the most obvious one to choose, it is pricey and many visitors may choose to seek accommodation away from the lake itself, particularly to the north or south of Lugano (following the railway line) where accommodation possibilities are numerous.

Lugano itself is in some ways a slightly staid resort, with wealthy, cosmopolitan residents and a large ex-patriot community. The peaks **Monte Brè** and **Monte San Salvatore** are both accessible by funicular from the town and offer easy walking in attractive countryside above the lake. Other excursions include a trip up **Monte Generoso** by rack railway; a visit to the model village of **Swissminiatur**; or tough walking (and in winter, good skiing) in the Monte Lema/Monte Tamaro area, west of the city.

Heading south across the border, **Como** (only forty minutes by train from Milan) is a thoroughly Italian city – shabby, inviting, and occasionally beautiful. Its huge lake runs north-south, like a stretched piece of ribbon, reaching from the north Italian plains to deep inside the Alps. The city is covered in the last part of this chapter, along with **Varese**, the other Italian centre most accessible from the Lugano area.

LUGANO

Lugano is the largest town in the Ticino and, after Zurich and Geneva, Switzerland's third most important financial centre – this is where rich northern Italians keep their money. Lugano is also one of Switzerland's most popular and most fashionable summer holiday resorts, and has been attracting Europe-wide attention since the opening of the St Gotthard railway in 1882.

There are a few specific sights to head for and also many museums, but many will be content with window-shopping and strolling in the lakeside gardens, immediately east of the centre.

Heading down into the town from the station, the nearest and most obvious landmark is the huge **cathedral of St Lawrence** (San Lorenzo). The façade dates from the Renaissance, and the interior betrays a Baroque revamp, but the building was originally a Romanesque construction which was greatly extended during the thirteenth and fourteenth centuries – the scratchy frescoes in the interior date back to the fourteenth century.

From here take the winding pedestrianised street that wends its way down to the centre of the town, almost entirely given away to visitors it seems, filled as it is with cafés, bars, restaurants and expensive souvenir shops. For a bit more local flavour pay a visit to the market held in the **Piazza della Riforma** every Tuesday and Friday morning. Anyone requiring a bit of mental stimulation may care to take on one of the locals at a game of pavement chess outside the Burger King – though it's not a good idea to put any money on it.

Lugano's other major church, **Santa Maria degli Angioli**, is situated next to the lake. It was built for the Franciscans in the early sixteenth century and is most remarkable for its engrossing frescoes by Bernardino Luini, Leonardo's finest student, painted while he was a guest of the friars here towards the end of his life.

(*See* pages 104/105 for details of Lugano's museums).

MONTE BRÈ

It takes about twenty minutes to travel from the bottom funicular station on Via Pico up to the peak of Monte Brè (3,035ft/925m). The village of **Brè**, a fifteen minute walk further on, is quite picturesque and boasts a very interesting museum devoted to painter Wilhelm Schmid (1892-1971) – indeed the village seems to play host to a number of budding artists with frescoes, paintings and pretty tiled designs adorning many a wall.

Walks from Brè take you back down to Lugano (1hr 50min) or Gandria (50min), or even on to Alpe Bolla or Mount Boglia for those feeling a bit more adventurous. Alternatively, there is a restaurant in Brè for those just in need of a sit down.

• SELECTED WALK •

MONTE BRÈ TO SORAGNO

This is a fairly easy walk, taking around three hours, which runs from the top station of the Monte Brè funicular to Soragno, a village north of Lugano. It passes through forests and across some open pasture land, and never goes very high, which means it is safely open from Easter to November. There are no steep ascents and the paths are well-made and well-signposted throughout.

From the funicular station, head for the village of Brè, then into the trees to Carbonera (after one hour) and then Alpe Bolla, a farm/restaurant complex situated amidst trees and pastureland. From here retrace your steps a little way then head for the restaurant at Preda Grossa, and continue on down to Colorino and then Soragno, for buses back to Lugano.

EAST FROM LUGANO INTO ITALY

Due east from Lugano a road runs along the lake shore via the picturesque fishing village of **Gandria** and then across the Italian border to **Porlezza**, the lake's easternmost extremity. Beyond here the road continues to **Menaggio** on Lake Como. Gandria and Porlezza can both be reached by boat from Lugano. There are also three buses per day which ply the Lugano-Gandria-Porlezza-Menaggio route, leaving from the via S.Balestra bus station in Lugano and also calling in at Lugano station. These buses reach Menaggio in an hour from Lugano, and continue on to the Italian mountain resort of Chiavenna and thence back into Switzerland and the fashionable ski resort of St Moritz (a total of four hours travelling time from Lugano).

Gandria

Clinging to the steep sides of the lake east of Lugano is Gandria, a former fishing village, but now one of the most visited lakeside settlements and best seen from a boat approaching across the water. The fading pastel-coloured houses, with red and green shutters and reddish, sagging roofs, seem about to tumble into the lake, and the whole place has a very Italian air about it. Nowadays, tourism, rather than fishing, is the primary activity here, with the smart restaurants in the village feeding the boatloads of visitors who land at the quay throughout the day in summer. It's undeniably a beautiful place, but apart from eating and drinking at pricey eating houses there's not

(cont'd on page108)

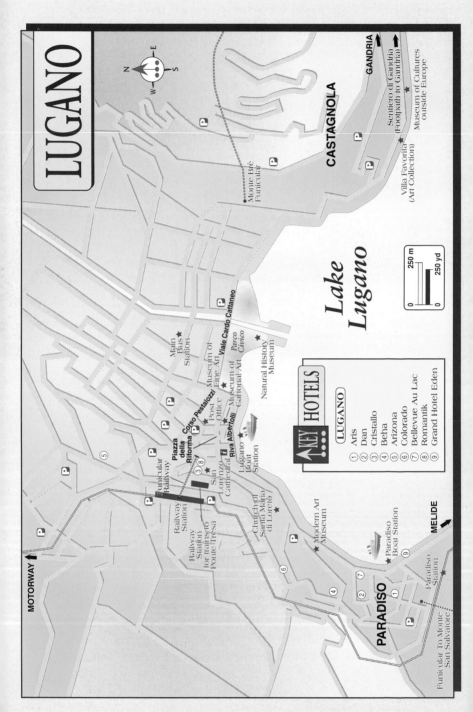

LUGANO

N W E S

MOTORWAY

Railway Station

Railway Station
for trains to
Ponte Tresa

Funicular
Railway

Piazza
della
Riforma

Corso Pestalozzi

Post
Office

Museum of
Fine Art

Museum of
Cantonal Art

Viale Carlo Cattaneo

Main
Bus
Station

Riva Albertolli

San
Lorenzo
Cathedral

Lugano
Boat
Station

Church of
Santa Maria
di Loreto

Parco
Civico

Natural History
Museum

Monte Brè
Funicular

CASTAGNOLA

GANDRIA

Sentiero di Gandria
(Footpath to Gandria)

Villa Favorita
(Art Collection)

Museum of Cultures
outside Europe

Lake
Lugano

250 m
250 yd

Modern Art
Museum

Paradiso
Boat Station

PARADISO

Paradiso
Station

MELIDE

Funicular To Monte
San Salvatore

HOTELS

LUGANO

1 Aris
2 Dan
3 Cristallo
4 Beha
5 Arizona
6 Colorado
7 Bellevue Au Lac
8 Romantik
9 Grand Hotel Eden

Above: Piazza Riforma, Lugano
Below: Gardens in Lugano

Cars and Motorbikes Museum
(Esposizione Veicoli d'Epoca)
Via Maraini 46,
Lugano – Pregassona
Located in the northern suburbs of the city, this museum houses an unusual collection of more than one hundred motorbikes and cars from the earliest models to the 1970s. Open: November-April only, Sundays only 2-5pm.

Museum of Cantonal Art
Via Canova 10
This museum comprises three former palaces and houses painting and sculpture collections from largely the nineteenth and twentieth centuries. Alongside contemporary Ticinese artists are works by Turner, Degas, Renoir and Pissaro. Open: Tuesdays 2-5pm; Weds-Sun 10am-5pm.

Museum of Cultures Outside Europe
Via Cortivo 24
This museum is housed in an ornate Neo-classical lakeside villa, the Villa Helenum in Castagnola, a short bus ride east of Lugano. Created in 1985 through the generosity of Serge and Graziella Brignoni, the museum comprises a collection of beautifully painted and fashioned masks and wooden figures from tribal regions of Asia, Africa and Oceania, pieces which are sometimes known as 'primitive art'. This unusual museum will be of particular interest to those interested in the anthropology and ethnography of these regions. To reach it, take bus 1 from by the fountain by the lake in the centre of Lugano, to San Domenico; the museum is a ten-minute walk along the road which runs along the shore of the lake from here. It is also a stop on a number of boat routes. The *Sentiero di Gandria* footpath also runs past it. Open: Wednesday-Sunday, 10am-5pm.

Museum of Fine Arts
Parco Civico
Works by Swiss and European artists from the fifteenth to the nineteenth centuries, housed in a nineteenth century villa in the city park. Open: 10am-noon, 2-6pm, daily except Monday.

Museum of Modern Art
Riva A. Caccia 5
Largely known for its temporary exhibitions of modern art; plus a permanent collection of works by Ticinese artists, and by Rousseau, Monet and Pissarro.
Open: 10am-noon, 2-6pm, daily except Monday; no lunch time closing at weekends.

Natural History Museum
Palazzo degli Studi, Parco Civico
Fossils, rocks, minerals and flora from the Ticino region.
Open: 9am-noon, 2-5pm, daily except Sunday, Monday.

Swiss Customs Museum
On lake shore, Cantine di Gandria
This isn't the most obviously appealing subject for a museum, but a visit to the old customs house, Cantine di Gandria, and its exhibition relating to the borders of Switzerland and their control, is actually quite absorbing. The museum can only be reached by boat (or by walking from Campione) and is located on the shores of the lake opposite Gandria, to the east of Lugano. There are mock-ups of border posts in the nineteenth century, displays of the former tools of a custom officer's trade, and pieces relating to modern day issues of customs control, including apprehension of drug smugglers and of false passport holders. The borders of Switzerland are drawn across mountain ranges, lakes and farmland, and the museum details how these areas have been patrolled and protected through the ages. Unfortunately there's only a minimum amount of information in English. Unusually, there's no entry charge. Open: April-October, daily 1.30-5.30pm.

Villa Favorita – the Thyssen-Bornemisza Collection
Castagnola
One of the largest private art galleries in Europe, specialising in European and American paintings from the nineteenth and twentieth centuries; unfortunately all the Old Masters were transferred to Spain back in 1992, but there's still a varied and impressive collection here. Take bus no. 1 from the fountain in central Lugano, or a short ride by boat from the pier. Very close to the Museum of Cultures Outside Europe (see above). Open: Friday, Saturday, Sunday only; 10am-5pm.

Gandria

Menaggio, on Lake Como

LUGANO & COMO

Capanna Tamaro
Monte Tamaro
Monte Gradiccioli
Birönico
Alpe Foppa
BELLINZONA

Monte Lema

PORLEZZA
MENAGGIO
LAKE COMO

Monte Boglia
Soragno
Preda Grossa
Colorino
Alpe Bolla
Carbonera
Monte Brè

Miglieglia
Astano   Novaggio
Cademario
LUGANO
Cassarate Gandria
Malcantone

Sessa
Agno
Castagnola

Paradiso

Cantine
di Gandria
Swiss Customs
Museum

LUINO /
LAKE
MAGGIORE

Lake Lugano

Brè

Monte San
Salvatore

Campione
d'Italia

Ponte Tresa
Carona

Melide
Swissminiatur

Monte
Generoso

Brusino-
Arsizio
Monte
S. Giorgio
Melano

Mercote
*Lake
Lugano*
Serpiano
Bellavista
Muggio

Riva
San Vitale
Capolago

Porto
Ceresio
Meride

ITALY

MENDRISIO

Mendrisiotto

VALLE DI MUGGIO

Balerna
*Lake
Como*

CHIASSO

VARESE

MILAN

Brunate

COMO

MILAN

N
W   E
S

KEY
.... Cable Car
.... Walks
•••••••••• Rack rly

0 ———— 3 miles
0 ———— 3km

actually that much to do here. The *Sentiero di Gandria* is a very popular footpath which runs from here to Castagnola, near Lugano.

Menaggio

The Italian resort of Menaggio on Lake Como is a place for lying on the beach, strolling, eating, drinking and very little else. This is not a destination, so much as a stop on the way, or a base to explore the tiny villages in the surrounding hills or the valley of the Senagra stream. The tourist office has details of walks in the area, the best being the ascent up to Monte Bregagno (6,913ft/2,107m) – or there's a golf course just above the town for those that way inclined (☎ 32103).

SOUTH FROM LUGANO

The rocky, steep-sided peninsula south of Lugano, where a bulky tongue of land juts south between two arms of the lake, has been a justifiably popular point for excursions from the resort since the nineteenth century. **Monte San Salvatore**, a towering, steep-sided mass of rock, rises distinctively to the south of the city. It is reached by a well-patronised cable railway, and has an excellent viewpoint over the lake.

Beyond San Salvatore small, quiet, villa-strewn villages are linked by paths through the woods and by minor roads, and the crowds thin out, making this a good place for easy walks. From the summit, many head for either **Morcote**, the picturesque village at the southern end of the peninsula, or **Melide**, on its eastern side; the latter is the location for **Swissminiatur**, an engrossing model village where the distinctive sights and buildings of Switzerland have been reconstructed at waist-high level.

Monte San Salvatore

The summit of **Monte San Salvatore** (2,992ft/912m) is reached by a two-stage funicular railway that runs up from a station in Paradiso, reached by bus, train, boat or on foot from the centre of Lugano. The mainline railway station (Lugano-Paradiso) is a short distance from the lower station of the funicular (and situated on the slopes slightly above it). The panoramic views from the top encompass Lugano, the mountains beyond it, and of course the lake, whose shimmering blue surface is disturbed only by steamers cutting a V-shaped swathe in the still waters behind them as they travel between the lakeside resorts. It's a beautiful spot, but it can get crowded in summer when the weather is good.

Besides the overpriced café at the top (which doesn't actually overlook the best part of the panorama), there are two nature trails to follow (with information in German and Italian only), one of which runs past the small museum to the church. The museum consists of two parts: upstairs there is a collection of fossils and minerals from the surrounding area; downstairs there is a collection documenting the history from medieval times of a devotional order, the Archfraternity of Good Death (*Arciconfraternita della Buona Morte*). Members of the fraternity wore characteristic white hoods and gowns and took it upon themselves to accompany those condemned to die to their place of execution. They would comfort the condemned before they died and would deal with their bodies after they had suffered death by decapitation or drowning. It's a small but unusual collection, housed in only one room, and well worth a look.

Beyond the museum the path snakes up through the trees to the church of San Salvatore, which has been in the hands of the Archfraternity since 1680. It's a tiny, austere building, and it occupies the highest point on the peninsula, not surprisingly allowing for the best views.

From Monte San Salvatore a well-trodden path heads south, through the woods, to **Carona**, a village with an attractive ancient square at its centre. Beyond the square the marked path follows the road, until one reaches a Gothic church, part of which is unusually built above and over the roadway. Here it is possible to carry on south to Morcote (see below) or to turn left, following narrow roads which snake down towards the lakeside at Melide.

Melide

Melide itself is not particularly attractive; it's a cramped, busy
(cont'd on page 113)

Swissminiatur

The model village has occupied this sunny, narrow ledge of land by Lake Lugano since 1959 and has seen twenty million visitors pass through its gates since that time. It's an absorbing place to spend an hour or so – children will delight in watching the trains buzz in and out of tunnels and across bridges, whilst adults will enjoy looking at the hundred or so models which the trains rumble past. All the models represent real places and sights in Switzerland and can be identified by means of the information booklet obtainable at the entrance.

Medieval parts of cities such as Basel and Neuchatel, the nineteenth century federal parliament building in Bern, the ancient city of Bremgarten with its medieval bridge across the river Reuss, and numerous multi-turreted castles and spire-laden churches, contrast with more modern aspects of Switzerland, such as the planes waiting on the tarmac at Zurich airport, the working mountain cableways and the docks on the river Rhein at Basel, providing landlocked Switzerland's only water link to the sea. Much of it is inescapably 'twee' – this is chocolate-box Switzerland writ small – but the place is undeniably good fun, and there's nowhere else like this in the country.

If you head round the back of the 'mountains', you can see an area where old models are repaired and new ones are built. There are also play areas and rides for children around the periphery of the model area, and a number of cafés and shops.

Above: Morcote is one of the most visited villages on Lake Lugano

Left: View from Monte Generoso, above Lake Lugano

Above: The rack and pinion railway up Monte Generoso

Below: Melide, on the shores of Lake Lugano

Above: Swissminiatur: a model village by the lake at Melide, where you can see all of Switzerland – in minature

Although there are a number of opportunities for walking in the hills above Lake Lugano, allowing for good views over it, walking tracks which run along the lakeshore are few and far between. Most of the lakeshore is occupied by private villas, roads and railways, boating clubs and hotels, and so is inaccessible; the two walking paths described below, however, allow walkers access to the lakeshore east of Lugano.

1 GANDRIA TO CASTAGNOLA

The **Sentiero di Gandria** is an easy, paved footpath which runs along the lake, just above shore level, from the fishing village of Gandria to Castagnola, an eastern suburb of Lugano. Walking time is around thirty minutes. In Gandria the path is signposted from the top of the steps by the landing stages; it emerges in Castagnola by the San Domenico bus stop on the main Gandria-Lugano road (served by Lugano municipal bus line 1 from the fountain in the centre of town). In Castagnola the route passes by the entrance to the Museum of Cultures Outside Europe and there are a couple of smart restaurants along its length with terraces overlooking the lake.

2 CAMPIONE D'ITALIA TO CANTINE DI GANDRIA

This is a longer and more difficult walk, taking a little under two hours. It runs around the heavily wooded and very steep shores of the lake opposite Lugano, from Campione d'Italia to the customs museum at Cantine di Gandria. Both Cantine and Campione have boat landing stages; there is no road access to Cantine.

From the landing stage at Campione, head up the hill past the apartment blocks to the Via Pugerna, which is a path leading from the upper part of the town into woodland. This first part is difficult to navigate – if the tourist office is open, ask for their free map. Otherwise, from the landing stages, take the Via Bezzola, the Corso Italia, the Corso Fratelli Fusina, and then the Via Totone, which leads to up to the Via Pugerna (after the third hairpin). When the Via Pugerna emerges from woodland onto a road, follow signs down to Caprino and then to Cantine.

The second half of the walk is on a path which sometimes touches the shoreline, and at other times runs through woods a little way above the lake. It's recommended only for the nimble-footed as there are several rocky landslides to cross (which sometimes cause the path to be closed). The path passes a *grotto* just past Caprino and then several deserted, boarded-up boat houses before reaching the grotti situated just along the shoreline from the customs museum at Cantine (see page 105).

place, squeezed onto a tiny area of flat land by the lake. Situated at the western end of the causeway, which carries the main Gotthard road and railway line across Lake Lugano, it is swamped by the noise of traffic and trains. It takes an hour or so of easy, downhill walking to get there from San Salvatore via Carona, and there are plenty of train and boat links back to Lugano from here. Its principal attraction is **Swissminiatur**, a popular model village sandwiched between the station and the lake (see page 109).

Morcote

From Monte San Salvatore it takes around two hours of fairly easy walking to reach Morcote; at the southern tip of the peninsula, it's also linked by boat and bus to Lugano and Melide. Morcote's beautiful setting at the foot of the steep slopes of Monte Arbostora, the well preserved streets and buildings, a couple of fine churches and an elegant park make it one of the most visited and attractive lakeside settlements after Lugano.

In the village itself there is the **chapel of San Antonio di Padova** (1676), and a beautifully laid-out garden, the **Parco Scherrer**,

Church of Sant Maria del Sasso

Morcote is dominated by the Santa Maria del Sasso church, which is linked to the lower part of the village by a flight of 408 stone steps (the path from Carona passes it before heading down into the village). Founded in the thirteenth century, the church was rebuilt in 1462 and was remodelled again, this time in Baroque style, in 1758, when the campanile was added. The wall frescoes date from the sixteenth century.

created in the 1930s and named after its designer. Rising above the lake on a series of terraces, this ornamental garden is home to many species of sub-tropical plants, and is a delight for keen botanists.

You can cross by boat from Morcote to **Porto Ceresio** which faces Morcote on the Italian shores of the lake. There's nothing much to see at Ceresio, but from the railway station (opposite the steamer pier) you can catch a train to Varese and on to Milan.

WEST AND NORTH-WEST OF LUGANO

The **Malcantone** is an area of attractive villages and countryside situated between Lugano and the Italian border. It's here that some of the most unspoiled and characteristic villages of the Ticino are situated. From one of them,

Miglieglia, a cable car runs up to skiing grounds at the summit of Monte Lema, which is the finishing point for a very popular half-day walk from the summit of Monte Tamaro, further north.

ALPE FOPPA TO MONTE LEMA VIA MONTE TAMARO

This is one of the most popular walks in the whole of the Ticino and on clear days in summer the path is always busy with walkers. The route, which takes around four hours and is steep in places, runs from the top station of the Bironico-Alpe Foppa cable car to the summit of Monte Lema, from where there's a cable car down to Miglieglia in the Malcantone.

The walk is so popular that at **Bironico** it's possible to buy one ticket which combines a ride from Bironico to Alpe Foppa, a ride at the end of the walk from Monte Lema to Miglieglia, and a return

shuttle bus trip from Miglieglia to Bironico. This ticket can also be bought at most Ticino rail stations, combined with a rail ticket to Rivera-Bironico station on the Bellinzona-Lugano line.

There's no water along the route (beyond Capanna Tamaro) so bring plenty with you. Bear in mind that it can also get very hot when the sun comes out as the slopes are very exposed and for most of the way there is no shade. Paths are well made and signposted throughout. As the walk does not rise above 6,560ft (2,000m) at any point, and because of its southerly location, it's free of snow for a longer period than many other walks described in this book, and is passable from around May to November.

Monte Tamaro

From **Bironico** village, on the main Lugano-Bellinzona road, a cable car runs up to **Alpe Foppa** which gives spectacular views over Bellinzona and across to the mountains of the northern Ticino. The lower station of the cable car is a five to ten minute walk from Rivera-Bironico station, a stop for local train services operating on the

Bellinzona-Lugano-Chiasso route.

By the top station is a remarkable building, a modern church (which doesn't look anything like a church from the outside) designed by Mario Botta, the region's most noted modern architect. It's a striking construction, celebrating its altitude and stunning location through curving terraces set on different levels, and crenellations and stairways which echo the rocky

Above: View from Monte Tamaro to Monte Lema walk over Lake Maggiore and the Italian Alps

Opposite: The summit of the Monte Tamaro cable car

From the top of the cable car station at Alpe Foppa (see text), follow the vehicle track to Capanna Tamaro (40min) and then the path on to the summit of Monte Tamaro (another 40min). The last twenty minutes of the ascent is steep but there are outstanding views during most of this first section of the route. The path runs back down from the summit to a ridge, from where it ascends steeply to Monte Gradiccioli. From here you can see the summit of Monte Lema, with its restaurant and skiing facilities, but it's further than it looks, and takes another two hours to reach. The final forty minutes or so involve a fairly steep descent to a vehicle track, which then rises steeply up towards the restaurant next to the top cable car station. Miglieglia, the lower station of the Monte Lema cable car, is an attractive village, with a bus service to Lugano in addition to the shuttle bus service back to Bironico.

mountain scenery in which it is set. The interior is surprisingly stark and bare, with no furnishings beyond the merely functional.

From the top cable car station it's a walk of forty minutes along a vehicle track to the **Capanna Tamaro**, a mountain hut set on a narrow ledge. It has some of the most stunning views in the Ticino, encompassing Lake Maggiore, Lake Lugano and high mountains to the north and west, such as the snow-covered bulk of the Monte Rosa. Beyond the capanna a path cut into the hillside rises after a further forty minutes to the summit of **Monte Tamaro**, the setting for the most spectacular views. Paths run down from here to a low pass on the road from Vira, on the southern shore of Lake Maggiore, to Indemini (the route so far described is also the first part of the popular Alpe Foppa to Monte Lema walk, *see* previous pages).

The Malcantone

The Malcantone is an area of attractive, unspoiled and very quiet villages set amidst wooded, hilly countryside due west of Lugano. It's said that the degree of architectural preservation of these villages is unmatched anywhere else in the Canton. Typically they have narrow, winding car-less lanes which creep up hillsides past ancient churches and houses surrounding courtyards. The area is best seen with a car, but there are bus routes around the villages beginning in Lugano,

or in Ponte Tresa, on the western arm of the lake, reached by metre-gauge train from Lugano (the terminus is outside the main station) or by boat.

Specific villages to head for include: **Miglieglia**, the lower terminus for the cable car to Monte Lema, the closest skiing grounds to Lugano and the location for some magnificent views; **Novaggio** and the health resort of **Cademario**; further south, **Astano** is a hill-top resort, surrounded by chestnut forests; due south of here is **Sessa**, the former administrative centre of the region, where there's a fifteenth century governor's residence on the square, and ornate wood carvings in the church.

SOUTH-EAST OF LAKE LUGANO –
THE MENDRISIOTTO

The **Mendrisiotto** is the southernmost tip of the Ticino (and of Switzerland), at the apex of the arrow head shape formed by the canton as it juts into northern Italy. This is where the mountains end and the plains of northern Italy begin to open up. The two main centres, Mendrisio and Chiasso, are surrounded by light industry, low wooded hills and extensive areas of vineyards, which produce a large quantity of Ticino's wine.

The main attractions of the Mendrisiotto are the cog railway up Monte Generoso and the cable car up to Serpiano, both giving access to good hiking areas. The Valle Muggio, which is accessible from Chiasso, is a scenic valley right on the country's most southerly tip and makes for a pretty, if brief, detour.

The area can easily be visited from Lugano, as Mendrisio is around thirty minutes from Lugano by train (and even less by road), although Mendrisio itself would make a good base for those wishing to explore the area in more detail.

Mendrisio & Chiasso

Mendrisio is the chief administrative town of the region and has been an important political centre since medieval times. Today the town has a modern appearance, although there are a few interesting old buildings in the centre, such as the nineteenth century **church of SS Cosma and Damiano**, and the **Palast der Edelleute Rusca**, the former fifteenth century courthouse.

· CAMPIONE D'ITALIA ·

Campione d'Italia, which lies south-east of Lugano facing Monte San Salvatore, is a geopolitical oddity – an area of Italian territory which is wholly surrounded by Switzerland. This unique situation arises from a quirk of medieval history. The settlement was an independent fiefdom with allegiance to the Bishop of Milan, and as the Swiss Confederacy gradually gained control of the Ticino during the eighteenth century, the town remained resolutely loyal to its traditional ties. At the Congree of Vienna in 1815, when the present-day boundaries of Switzerland were fixed, the border was drawn carefully around Campione to make it a geographical 'island', much to the annoyance of the Swiss delegation.

The situation remains unchanged, and nowadays Campione is a strange mixture of Swiss and Italian. The place is fastidiously neat and tidy, goods are priced in Swiss francs and most of the cars are registered in the Ticino, but the banks around the main square are all Italian, and law and order is in the hands of the *carabinieri*, the Italian state police force. The Post Office sells Italian stamps but they must be bought with Swiss currency.

The only access to the town is through Swiss territory, by boat or road from Lugano. There have been plans for decades to build a cable car up the slope above Campione, linking the settlement with the ridge above it, which is in Italy, but all these plans seem to have come to nothing.

The Italian *tricolore* flies above the landing stages for boats (there are no passport checks), which opens into the Piazza Roma, the main square. Just up the hill from the square is an office of the Italian State Tourist Board which provides a useful free map for visitors.

In truth, though, there's not actually a lot to see here: Campione consists mostly of apartment blocks and hotels, which rise up along steeply twisting roads from the lakeside. The **Casinò Municipale** is popular with well-healed visitors from the other side of the lake, but the only specific sight of any interest is the Chiesa di Santa Maria dei Ghirli, a ten minute walk from the Piazza Roma (turn right and keep walking beside the lake). The church is a quiet haven of sanctuary, built above the lakeshore with its own private landing stage. The interior has mainly Baroque decorations, including eighteenth century frescoes depicting the *Last Judgement* and the *Garden of Eden*; other frescoes are earlier and have been dated to the fourteenth century.

Unless you're in the Ticino during Easter, when the town stages its centuries-old Maundy Thursday procession (ask at tourist offices for details), Mendrisio can be safely ignored, as can Chiasso, further south, Switzerland's lowest and most southerly town.

For centuries Chiasso has been an important transit and customs point, and nowadays there's a frontier crossing into Italy at one end of the main street; passports are still checked here, an unusual occurrence in a Europe where boundaries are assuming less and less importance. Immediately beyond the frontier post are the shabby northern suburbs of Como. A large chunk of Chiasso is occupied by railway sidings, as this is the terminus of many trains which run south from Zurich and Basel through the Gotthard to Bellinzona

The Valle di Muggio

The Valle di Muggio is an attractive valley running north from Chiasso between bare, low hills dotted with tiny villages whose houses have distinctive red-tiled roofs. The valley is very quiet, largely because the road is a dead end which means that traffic here is very light. Although it's possible to travel between Chiasso and **Muggio**, at the head of the valley, by bus or car, a better way of appreciating this area is on foot. A number of paths run down from Bellavista and Monte Generoso into the valley in addition to shorter paths which link the hamlets along its length.

Muggio

Top: Looking south from above Campione
Above: Sessa, Malcantone

and Swiss slopes, and feeding on grass, shrubs and leaves.

Serpiano & Meride

From the tiny lakeside hamlet of **Brusino-Arsizio**, a stop for boats on Lake Lugano as they chug between Melide and Morcote, a cable car runs up to Serpiano, from where there's a wonderful view over the southern section of the lake. There's a restaurant at the top of the cable car and a walk of fifteen minutes along a level path through trees leads from the cable car station to the plush Hotel Serpiano. From the hotel's terrace there's another good view, this time with the picturesque village of Morcote clearly visible. The hotel is also at the end of a bus route running up from Mendrisio station, via Meride.

Meride itself, situated in rolling hills to the north-west of Mendrisio, is a quiet, unspoiled village with narrow alleyways along which houses with inner courtyards and loggias cluster. In the fossil museum here there are various petrified skeletons of creatures found in the surrounding area, especially saurians, which have been found in rich abundance on the nearby Monte San Giorgio.

• SELECTED WALK •

SERPIANO TO MERIDE VIA MONTE SAN GIORGIO

Most of this walk is through woodlands and although it does not rise particularly high, the path up Monte San Giorgio, which is the highest point between the two southerly 'arms' of Lake Lugano, is steep and slippery in places — after rain it can be quite dangerous as the path gets very muddy. As the area receives comparatively little in the way of snow, due to its southerly, low-altitude location, this walk can be completed virtually all year round.

From the cable car station at Serpiano, follow the signs to Monte San Giorgio; the first twenty minutes, on a broad, level path, is easy, and leads to a nice grotto. From here the route begins to climb; the ascent, almost wholly through woods, is steep and slippery in places, and fences have been built at some points to help walkers navigate the route. After around an hour the path emerges at the summit of Monte San Giorgio, where there's a good view over the lake and the surrounding countryside.

The path down to Meride from the summit takes a little over an hour and, for the most part, runs along a well-made cobbled path that runs down through thick, peaceful woodland. Some of it is marked off as a nature trail but the information boards are in Italian only. There are buses from Meride up to the Hotel Serpiano, near the cable car top station, and to Mendrisio, on the main Lugano-Chiasso rail line.

COMO

It is a matter of one's own personal taste whether one's impression of Como is of a slightly tatty lakeside town or a gently peeling, highly evocative historic centre – much depends on one's instincts about the relative merits of Switzerland and Italy. Como certainly isn't Italy's most charismatic centre but relative to the Ticino it has an agreeably unfussy air, and in the summer months it is very much on the backpackers' itinerary as they traverse the continent in time-honoured fashion.

History

Settlement in these parts stretches back to prehistoric times and the walls that surround the Old City reflect the layout of the Roman town, indeed under the Romans Como developed into a strategically vital and economically prosperous town. Since then its political fortunes have ebbed and flowed, being nearly destroyed in the early twelfth century during the Ten Years War with Milan and suffering long periods of rule by Spain, Austria and France. Its economic base, since its inception in 1510, has been the silk industry which busily supplies the Milanese fashion gurus.

The Old City

The central orientation point of Como is the lakeside square **Piazza Cavour**. It's a defiantly modern-looking square, but then it was only created in 1872 when the old port area was filled in. Boat trips around the lake leave from here. A yellow 'M' sign entices you out of the square along the arcaded Via Plinio which leads you to Piazza Duomo which, as the name suggests, plays host to the city's cathedral.

Central Como

The Duomo & Broletto

Work originally began on the **cathedral** *(duomo)* in 1396, though construction was not in fact completed until the eighteenth century when the magnificent dome was added. As a consequence the building encompasses a unique cross-section of architectural styles. The almost overwhelming late-gothic façade dates to 1455-86, the two scholarly-looking gentlemen flanking the main doorway are the Plinys Elder and Younger, both great classicists who originated from the city. A pamphlet is available indoors for a more detailed description of the interior, or for L1000 you can plug yourself into a pre-recorded appreciation.

To the left of the cathedral as you view it from the square is the adjoining, though completely unrelated **Broletto** which actually dates to 1215 and so therefore pre-dates the cathedral – indeed the Broletto lost two of its arches as a result of the building work. This was originally the seat of the city council, though in the eighteenth century it was turned into a theatre. Subsequently it has been used as a record office and exhibition hall. In 1972 the Broletto was restored to its original appearance. The rough-looking tower looks old but was almost completely rebuilt in 1927.

Now leave Piazza Duomo along Via Vittorio Emanuele, one of the city's most attractive shopping streets. Follow the signs that lead you to Piazza St Fedele which is dominated by the **basilica of St Fedele**. The interior is either interminably gloomy or highly evocative depending on your state of mind. The square itself served as the forum back in Roman times and at the end of the nineteenth century it was a grain market. A couple of the buildings on the square are definitely showing their age from the condition of their wooden structures – these date back to the sixteenth century.

Walk now down Via Odescalchi, and then take a left turn into Via Giovio, which eventually leads you to the Piazza Medaglie d'Oro Comasche. The piazza is home to the prosaically named **civic museum**, devoted to worthy collections of art and archaeology, and Como's **history museum**. As an aside, the town's most famous product – silk – has its own museum a quarter of an hour walk from the Old City on Via Valleggio.

Exit the square along Via Balestra which leads you to one of the great towers of the Old City wall, turn immediately right once through here, a very lively market is held along this street on Tuesday, Thursday and Saturday mornings.

Head back into the Old City through the next towering gate along Porte Torre (literally 'tower gate') into Via Cesare Cantù, then take the second left from here down Via Giovo. After about 110yd (100m) you'll come to a small sqaure dominated by a the daunting façade of the Palazzo

Volpi, a former courthouse now used to house various temporary art exhibitions. A short walk on along Via Giovo will bring you to Via Alessandro Volta, the richest quarter of Old Como as witnessed by the lengthy succession of elegant nineteenth century dwellings. A relaxing stroll down here will eventually bring you back to the lakeside.

From Piazza Cavour to Villa Olmo

Walking from Piazza Cavour, with the lake on your right, you will soon enter a park area. To the left an unusual looking monument can be seen, created in honour of the European Resistance Movement – a glass case contains stones from all the Nazi concentration camps.

Continue on and you will soon come across an oddly grand-looking building. This is a temple dedicated to the memory of Como's most famous son **Alessandro Volta**, local dignitary and physicist extraordinaire from whose name we derive the word 'volt'. The building was erected to celebrate the centenary of his death in 1927 and is in many ways more interesting than the exhibits contained within – an assortment of paintings, busts, documents and curios relating to the great man.

A little further along the waterfront is a huge war memorial built in 1933 and apparently based on designs for a hydro-electric power station. You may have been noticing whilst on your stroll a number of seaplanes taking off and landing on the lake, the explanation for this will be clear when you pass the next large building on the lakeside, an enormous aircraft hanger, in fact the only seaplane pilot school in Europe.

The remainder of the lakeside walk takes you past a succession of impressive villas, built in the eighteenth and nineteenth centuries by the city's most prosperous citizens. The last and most famous is the **Villa Olmo**, set in a small park and constructed in 1782-97 on the site of an elm tree, said to have been planted by Pliny the Younger himself. The building is owned by the council and is used to house various city functions and exhibitions, thus one can only visit the interior during one of these – though one is free to relax in the surrounding gardens.

The funicular to Brunate

A short walk around the other side of the lake from Piazza Cavour is a funicular railway that leads up to the small settlement of Brunate, a very popular excursion for visitors to the city since the service's inception in 1894. Departures are frequent (up to midnight in summer) and the journey time is a mere seven minutes. Admittedly once up the top there's not a great deal to do except savour the views so you may wish to lengthen your trip with a half-hour walk up to St Maurizio, which is dominated by a tall octagonal tower, the so-called Volta Lighthouse. The view from the top is breathtaking and apt to induce giddiness. Anyone intent on a serious day's hike could then continue on to Boletto, Bolettone or San Primo.

VARESE

Varese, 11 miles (18km) west of Como, turns its back on the lakes and mountains and is architecturally and historically tied to Milan and the Lombardy Plain. The town lies in the heart of the **Varesotto**, a wealthy region crammed with light industry and commuter settlements for Milan. It's a stylish place, with very pleasant formal gardens and excellent shopping, and in April and October it is busy with visitors to the Milan fashion shows which are held at this time. During the rest of the year there are far fewer visitors here than in Como, giving the town more of a genuine Italian feel.

The centre of the town is not particularly picturesque, combining grey-block 1930s architecture with prettier older corners, and its attractions lie more in its excursions and shopping rather than its sights, and the fact that it also makes an excellent stopping-off place between Milan (or Malpensa Airport) and the Ticino.

Getting there

Varese is less than thirty minutes away by train from Porto Ceresio (a stop for boats at the southern end of Lake Lugano); can also be reached by bus from Mendrisio; by train or bus from Laveno (see page 74), on the Italian shores of Lake Maggiore; and less conveniently by train or bus from Como.

Its two railway stations are close to one another, separated by the Piazza Kennedy bus station – trains from Como use Varese Nord (change at Saronno and use Como Lago station in Como to travel this route). From the McDonald's restaurant opposite the Piazza Kennedy, take the Via Morosini, then the Via Veneto and the Corso Moro, to reach Piazza Monte Grappa, in the centre of town.

Central Varese

Like many Italian town centres, it seems initially that the streets of central Varese are lined mainly with banks, of which Italy has dozens. The main focal point is the **Piazza Monte Grappa**, dating mainly from the 1930s, with a modernist rectangular fountain and a rather brutal campanile-style tower. A much older and prettier campanile is near by and it marks the centre of old Varese. This 236ft (72m) high structure, dating from the seventeenth and eighteenth centuries, is the *Del Bernascone*, named after its architect, and distinguished by the fact that its design patterns change as the eye travels upwards.

Next to the campanile is the **basilica of St Vittore**, most of which dates from around 1600, although the façade is a Neo-classical addition a little more than two hundred years old. The square in front of the building, with its flagstones and high, pastel-shaded walls, studded with shuttered windows, is unmistakably Italian. The interior of the church is awash with rich decoration, including paintings, ornate wood carvings and sculpture; there are sixteenth century frescoes in the **Chapel of St Marta**. The smaller church next to the campanile is the **Baptistery of San Giovanni**, the oldest building in the city, solid and stately. Like many medieval churches it is built on the site of an older building, inside there is a font dating from the eighth century in addition to some fine thirteenth century frescoes.

Running off Piazza Monte Grappa, and linked by an arched passageway to the basilica, is the **Corso Matteotti**, a pedestrianised shopping street lined with elegant designer-wear shops, an excellent place to while away the time browsing, strolling and watching the world go by from one of the open-air restaurants.

Three minutes away on foot from the piazza, on Via Luigi Sacco, is a long pink building, the **Palazzo Estense**, an eighteenth-century residence of the Duke of Modena which is now the city hall. Its beautiful gardens, combining a grand fountain surrounded by immaculate lawns with more secluded, quieter ponds and gushing ornamental waterfalls, are a highlight of Varese.

At the far end of the gardens, the **Villa Mirabello** houses the city museum, exhibiting archaeological and historical collections and a butterfly collection of a local tenor; unfortunately there's no infor-mation in English. The oddest exhibit is the mummified body of a young boy, aged eleven or twelve, who died in around 1645 and lies in a glass case in a room all to himself.

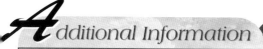

PLACES TO VISIT

Wilhelm Schmid Museum
Lugano-Brè
Open: 10am-noon, 2-5pm,
closed Monday and Tuesday.

Fossil Museum
Meride
Open: daily, 8am-6pm.

Swissminiatur
Melide
Open: mid-March to end of
October, 9am-6pm; may also
open during afternoons in
November and December
depending on weather.
☎ (091) 640 1060

Como

Art Gallery (Palazzo Volpi)
Open: Tuesday-Friday 9.30am-
12.30pm, 2-5pm; Sunday
10am-1pm.

Civic Museum
Open: Tuesday-Saturday 9.30am-
12.30pm, 2-5.30pm, mornings
only on Sunday; closed on
holidays.

Temple Voltiano
Open: Tuesday-Sunday 10am-
noon, 3-6pm; 4pm October-
March.

Silk Museum
Open: Tuesday-Saturday 9am-
noon, 3-6pm.

Varese

Villa Mirabello
Open: Tuesday-Saturday 9.30am-
12.30pm, 2-5.30pm, mornings
only on Sunday, closed on
holidays.

ACCOMMODATION

There's a huge range of places to stay in the Lugano region, and it's
best to choose somewhere with the help of a brochure of hotel listings
from tourist offices. The following is a tiny selection:

Swiss Youth Hostels
Association Youth Hostel
Via Cantonale 13, Lugano
☎ (091) 966 2728
Dormitory accommodation
and private rooms. Thirty
minutes walk uphill from
station or bus no.5.
Reception closed noon-3pm.

* Hotel della Posta
Piazza Grande, Morcote
☎ (091) 996 1127,
Fax (091) 996 1779
Typical Ticino house on the main

square in Morcote; surprisingly
cheap for its location.

* Villa Elena
Via Lugano, Ponte Tresa
☎ (091) 606 5871,
Fax (091) 606 3658
Budget option; Ponte Tresa
is linked by boat and train
to Lugano.

(cont'd overleaf)

(cont'd from previous page)

* Osteria del Ponte
Via Rinaldi 2, Mendrisio
☎ (091) 646 3296
Cheap hotel in Mendrisio, on
the Lugano-Chiasso rail route.

** Aris
Via Geretta 8, Lugano-Paradiso
☎ (091) 994 1478,
Fax (091) 994 6481
Fairly low-cost, pre-war hotel
close to the Monte San Salvatore
funicular in Paradiso.

** Dan Hotel
*Via Domenico Fontana 1,
Lugano-Paradiso*
☎ (091) 985 7030,
Fax (091) 985 7031. Tranquil,
small pension, close to the lake in
Paradiso, a suburb of Lugano.

** La Gondoletta
Lungolago Motta 40, Melide
☎ (091) 649 7761,
Fax (091) 649 4855
Small pension close to lake in
Melide; lake views; close to
Swissminiatur,

** Hotel Svizzero
Capolago, ☎ (091) 648 1975,
Fax (091) 648 1753
Small hotel in Capolago, a
lakeside village between
Lugano and Mendrisio.

** Conca d'Oro au Lac
*Riva Paradiso 7,
Lugano-Paradiso*
☎ (091) 994 3131,
Fax (091) 994 6982

*** Beha
Via Mazzini 22, Lugano
☎ (091) 994 1331,
Fax (091) 994 7167
Positioned near centre of Lugano
and lake; restaurant with garden.

*** Albatro
Via Cl. Maraini 8, Lugano
☎ (091) 921 0921,
Fax (091) 921 0927

*** Colorado Hotel
Via Maraini 19, Lugano
☎ (091) 994 1631,
Fax (091) 993 1266
e-mail: colorad@dial.eunet.ch
Fairly smart but featureless hotel in
central Lugano, close to the lake.

**** Bellevue au Lac
Riva A Caccia 10, Lugano-Paradiso
☎ (091) 994 3333,
Fax (091) 9941273
Family owned hotel, fifteen
minutes walk from central
Lugano; open air heated pool.

**** Romantik-Hotel Ticino
Piazza Cioccaro 1, Lugano
☎ (091) 922 7772,
Fax (091) 923 6278
Plush, small hotel, right in the
heart of Lugano.

***** Grand Hotel Eden
Riva Paradiso 1, Lugano-Paradiso
☎ (091) 985 9200,
Fax (091) 985 9250
e-mail: eden.gh@bluewin.ch
Magnificently luxurious hotel by
the lake at Paradiso.

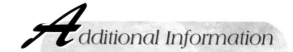

PUBLIC TRANSPORT

Air

Basel, Bern, Zurich and Geneva are all under fifty minutes from Lugano by air. The airport is at Agno, west of the city; shuttle buses from the railway station in Lugano.

Most services are operated by Crossair, a subsidiary of Swissair

Trains

Trains from Lugano: Bellinzona, 2 hourly (35min); Chiasso, 2 hourly (20-30min); Milan, hourly (90min); Como, hourly (50min); Zurich, hourly (3hrs 15min).

Lugano-Ponte Tresa by train: 2 hourly (20min).

Buses

The main bus station in Lugano is at Via Balestra in the city centre (see map on page 102). Many buses also call at the railway station.

Lugano-Miglieglia (cable car to Monte Lema): 9 daily (weekdays), 4-5 daily (holidays and Sundays) (1hr).

Morcote-Melide-Paradiso-Lugano: 2 hourly, (25min).

Mendrisio-Varese: 1-2 per hour; change at Gaggiolo (total journey time 50min), no Sunday service.

TOURIST INFORMATION

Lugano

Palazzo Civico, Riva Albertolli, ☎ (091) 913 3232, Fax (091) 922 7653 Open: April-October, 9am-6.30pm weekdays, 9am-12.30pm, 1.30pm-5pm Saturday, 10am-12pm, 2-4pm Sunday; November-March, 9am-12.30pm, 1.30-5.30pm, Mon-Fri only.

Other tourist offices are at the railway station and the airport. Website: www.lugano-tourism.ch

Other tourist offices in the area

Melide
☎ (091) 649 6383,
Fax (091) 649 5613

Caslano
Piazza Lago
☎ (091) 606 2986,
Fax (091) 606 5200

GETTING TO TICINO

By air

The only direct international flights into the Ticino are operated by **Crossair**, a subsidiary of Swissair, into Lugano airport at Agno, a short distance west of the city and linked to Lugano station by shuttle bus. Crossair fly direct to Lugano from London City airport. Their flights, however, are expensive and most travellers will fly into Zurich or Milan and proceed from there by train into the Ticino. Of the two, Milan is slightly closer, especially to the Lugano/Locarno region of the southern Ticino, but fares to Milan are slightly higher than Zurich fares.

Cheap flights from the UK or North America to Zurich or Milan can be obtained through discount flight centres which advertise in the travel sections of the national press, or the internet is, of course, a place to search for cheap flights.

Contact Swiss Travel Centres for information about sending luggage on from the airport to a final destination rail station; the same thing can be done by returning passengers, and Swissair will check in baggage for their travellers at Lugano and other main stations.

FLYING TO ZURICH

British Airways flies to Zurich (Kloten Airport) from Heathrow and Gatwick; **Swissair** operates routes from Heathrow, Birmingham and Manchester; **Crossair** has flights from Edinburgh, London (city), Manchester and Dublin; and **Air UK** flies from Stansted. A number of airlines in the proliferating low-cost market out of the UK also operate flights into Zurich, including **Go** and **Easyjet**.

Zurich airport is linked to Zurich HB (the main station in the city centre) by regular trains; there are hourly services from Zurich HB south to Bellinzona (for Locarno), Lugano and Chiasso.

Swissair flies into Zurich from Atlanta, Boston, Calgary, Chicago, Cincinati, Dallas/Fort Worth, Denver, Houston, Los Angeles, Miami, Montreal, New York, Orlando, Philadelphia, Salt Lake City, San Diego, San Francisco, Seattle, Tampa, Vancouver and Washington. Zurich is also served by a number of North American carriers.

FLYING TO MILAN

The Italian national carrier **Alitalia** runs direct services into Milan (Malpensa or Linate) from London, Dublin, Los Angeles, New York, San Francisco, Los Angeles, Miami, Montreal and Toronto.

North American carriers such as **Delta**, **TWA** and **American** also fly into Milan from American cities including New York, Chicago, Los Angeles and Miami.

British carriers including **BA** operate services from London, Manchester and other UK regional centres to Milan; **Go**, the low-cost offshoot of BA, operates flights from Stansted to Milan, and other 'no-frills' airlines are also opening up routes from the UK to Milan.

Of the two Milanese airports, Malpensa is the largest, a brand new, ultra-swish terminal for most intercontinental flights. It's located north-west of Milan and is actually slightly closer to Como and Chiasso than it is to Milan itself. There are around four buses per days from Malpensa to Chiasso and Lugano (ring ☎ (091) 807 8520 for details). Otherwise there are regular buses from both Malpensa, and Linate (the smaller airport located closer to the centre of Milan) to Milano Centrale station, from where there are trains more or less hourly into the Ticino (on the Milan-Como-Chiasso-Lugano-Bellinzona-Gotthard route). Note that some trains are fast *Cisalpino* services which are more expensive than ordinary services.

TELEPHONE NUMBERS FROM UK

Swissair and **Crossair**	☎ (020) 7434 7300
British Midland	☎ (0345) 554554
British Airways	☎ (0345) 222111
Alitalia	☎ (0870) 544 8259
Go	☎ (0845) 605 4321
	www.go-fly.com
STA Travel	☎ (020) 7937 9921
Trailfinders	☎ (020) 7938 3232
Campus Travel	☎ (020) 7730 3402
Easyjet	☎ (0870) 6000 0000
	www.easyjet.com

TELEPHONE NUMBERS FROM THE USA

Swissair and **Crossair**	☎ 1-800-221-4759
Alitalia	☎ 1-800-223-5730
Delta	☎ 1-800-241-4141
STA Travel	☎ 1-800-777-0112
Council Travel	
(discount tickets)	☎ 1-800-COUNCIL;
in New York	☎ (212) 822 2700

By train

With the proliferation of cheap airlines and flight deals, European rail travel has become comparatively expensive, and travelling by train to Switzerland is likely to work out more expensive than a journey by air. The exception is those who have rail passes, such as the Inter-rail under or over age 26 pass, or the Eurail pass (for non-European residents), or those under 26 who can buy BIJ youth tickets which give reductions on the normal fares. Information regarding times, prices and bookings is available from **Rail Europe**, ☎ (0870) 584 8848.

The best route between London and the Ticino involves travelling by **Eurostar** from London to Brussels, and picking up the overnight Brussels-Milan train which calls at Bellinzona, Lugano and Chiasso very early the next morning. A couchette (sleeping berth) on this train needs to be paid for over and above the cost of the main ticket; without any sort of reduction or pass the final cost can be as much as twice the cheapest air fares to Zurich or Milan.

The *Thomas Cook European Timetable* is published every month by Thomas Cook and is available from their branches, as a reference book in some libraries, and from booksellers. It gives the timings of virtually every train in Europe and is excellent for planning long distance rail journeys. In the USA it is available from the Forsyth Travel Library ☎ (800) 367 7984.

By coach

This is certainly the cheapest option as regards getting to Switzerland. **Eurolines** ☎ (01582) 404511, at 52 Grosvenor Gardens, near Victoria Coach Station in London, runs coaches from London to Basel in northern Switzerland (an overnight journey taking around 14 hours) from where there are regular trains to Lugano. Another alternative is their service to Milan, which takes 23 hours and runs via Paris.

By car

The distance by road from Calais to the Ticino is around 590 miles (950km). When planning journeys, bear in mind that motorways in France and Italy *(autoroutes/autostrada)* require tolls, whereas those in Germany *(autobahn)* do not. The likely point of entry to Swizterland for motorists from the UK is Basel, from where there is motorway access down to the Gotthard tunnel and thence the Ticino. This route passes through Lucerne, another very beautiful area of Switzerland.

Drivers should have a vehicle registration document, a green card (insurance certificate), a breakdown warning triangle and their own national driver's licence to drive a car into Switzerland. Also useful are a first aid kit, spare bulbs and a fire extinguisher. It might also be a good idea to take out a European breakdown assistance policy, issued by motoring organisations such as the AA ☎ (0800) 435980 or RAC (0870) 572 2722, which can give further information on driving to and in Switzerland. The RAC publishes an annual book, *European Motoring Guide*, useful for anyone driving to Switzerland.

TAXES & FEES

An annual motorway tax, known as the **vignette**, is levied on all vehicles using Swiss motorways. This must be purchased at border crossings (have cash ready) or in advance from Swiss Travel Centres (payment can be made by credit card and the vignette posted to you).

Caravans and trailers require an additional payment, but the fee for motorcycles is the same as the car drivers'. The vignette, which is actually a windscreen sticker, allows unlimited use of all Swiss motorways for a calendar year (if you buy the sticker in December you can use it until the end of the following year).

All motorways in Switzerland are identified by green signs. The Gotthard and San Bernardino tunnels, linking the Ticino with northern and north-eastern Switzerland respectively, are motorway tunnels and you must have paid the tax to use them.

ACCOMMODATION

Accommodation in the Ticino is plentiful, and information about prices and choices is easily obtainable. Accommodation options range from

campsites, youth hostels (in Lugano and Locarno), hotels in all catego-
ries, and huts in the mountains which are only reachable on foot. In
this book, accommodation options have been given at the end of each
chapter, but this is only a taster of what there is available (these listings do not include campsites but cover every other option).

Brochures detailing accommodation possibilities can be picked up
from tourist offices. There are four which cover the Ticino – Locarno
and the valleys, Lugano, the Mendrisio area in the far south, and the
upper Ticino (the latter covering chapters one, two and three). These
give an entry for every hotel, holiday apartment to rent, campsite and
mountain hut in that particular area, including phone and fax number,
e-mail contact, address, price and an idea of the facilities. Information
is given in English and maps are provided showing where hotels are
located.

Campsites

Campsites, administered by Touring Club der Schweiz (**TCS**, the national motoring organisation), are rated from one to five stars and are
really only useful for those with their own transport. Campsites tend to
operate only in summer and usually require advance reservation. There
is normally a price reduction with an International Camping Card
(obtainable from Camping and motoring organisations). The **Swiss
National Tourist Office** can supply a brochure listing all campsites in
the country.

Camping out in the mountains is technically illegal but no-one will
notice if you're discrete, although it is a good idea to ask farmers first
before pitching on their land.

Youth hostels

The youth hostels in Lugano and Locarno offer dormitory accommodation and are affiliated to the **Swiss Youth Hostels Association**. There's
an additional fee to pay for those who are not members of their own
Youth Hostels Association.

Mountain huts

Up in the mountains the huts run by the **Swiss** or **Ticino Alpine Clubs**
have rather spartan dormitory facilities with basic meals available. They
also tend to be quite pricey. However, they are rarely full and you will
not be turned away, but it might be a good idea to ring in advance to
see if the hostel is operating. Some places have no warden and payment is made on an 'honesty' system. There are mountain huts
(capannas) on walks described in Chapters one, two and four of this
book, but dozens are in operation across the Ticino.

Ristoranti con allogio

The cheapest options, beyond camping and the two youth hostels, are
the *ristoranti con allogio* – literally 'restaurants with rooms' (look out
for the word *camere* – rooms – or *zimmer frei*). There are dozens of

these throughout the Ticino, each one a restaurant with a few rooms for guests upstairs. They tend to be rated with no stars – bathroom facilities being rarely en-suite and usually located along the corridor.

Hotels

Increasing in price are the one, two, three, four, five and five star deluxe establishments (the latter confined to plush lakeside hotels in Lugano and Locarno, which come with their own private beaches). A hotel *garni* usually has limited cooking facilities for self-catering. All forms of accommodation are pricey by European standards, but the way of reducing costs is to stay away from the main centres (such as Lugano and Locarno). Remote, out-of-the-way places have some of the cheapest places to stay, although things can get difficult for those relying on public transport to reach them.

Most places include breakfast in the cost of the room; this is usually bread rolls, butter, cheese and jam in the cheaper places, with a buffet (including cold meats and cereals) in the more expensive places.

Apartments

Contact those listed in the accommodation brochures, or an agency such as **Interhome** (UK ☎ 020 8891 1294; USA ☎ 201 882 6864). **Swiss National Tourist Offices** have brochures detailing options for group accommodation, and for cheap student accommodation in towns.

Prices

The price of rooms varies according to season: high season on the lakes is summer, and in the mountains is winter. Prices are also in-creased during major festivals or events, such as in Locarno during the film festival. Most places will accept telephone reservations in advance – so long as you don't intend to arrive too late. In some places hotels give guests a 'Guest Card' which gives discounts on local museums, cable cars etc.

BANKS, CREDIT CARDS AND CURRENCY

The Swiss franc (*franco svizzero*; abbreviated to SF or CHF) is divided into one hundred units, known as *centesimi* to Italian-speakers. There are coins for five, ten, twenty and fifty (half franc coin) centisimi, and for one, two, and five francs; and notes for ten, twenty, fifty, one hundred, two hundred and a thousand francs. Switzerland is not a member of the EU and its currency will remain the Swiss franc as other European currencies are swallowed into the new pan-European Euro.

The franc is one of the strongest and most stable currencies in the world. Spending money in Switzerland is easy – it's one of the most expensive countries in the world for travellers – but thankfully obtain-ing money is easy, too. There are ATMs (hole-in-the-wall cash ma-chines) everywhere, usually attached to banks or post offices, or free-standing at railway stations. Cards issued in the UK or North America which have internationally-recognised symbols such as Visa or MasterCard can be used to obtain money at these machines, although no one machine will accept all cards, which can occasionally make looking for an appropriate machine frustrating.

Centres such as Lugano, Locarno, Bellinzona and Chiasso are crammed full of banks, but elsewhere there might only be one branch which may not have an ATM machine which takes your card – for this reason it is a good idea to bring a stock of travellers' cheques too. Internationally recognised banks, such as Credit Suisse and Union Bank of Switzerland (UBS), and branches of smaller banks too, are open from around 8.30am to 4.30pm Monday to Friday. Most railway stations also have a counter for changing cash or travellers' cheques, which is open long hours and at weekends, but they will not give cash advances on credit cards. Hotels will change money too, but take a high commission, which banks and stations don't charge.

Credit cards are taken by most hotels and restaurants (though not the cheaper one-star places). Credit and debit cards issued overseas in countries such as the UK can be used in machines at stations to buy train tickets, and even in public telephone booths instead of phone cards. In any case, check whether your card can be used before making a purchase.

The most widely-used card is the Eurocard. Eurocheques are used widely and money can be obtained from banks with a Eurocheque card. For expensive purchases over SF500, non-Swiss citizens can claim back the consumer tax (VAT) which they will have paid on their goods: get the shop to fill in any required paperwork, and then claim the tax back when leaving Zurich airport or at main border crossings, or even by post after you get home.

CLIMATE

Winter often sees the most stable weather in the Ticino, with clear, cold skies for days on end which make for excellent skiing conditions. This weather can last up until Easter, when it is very often warm and sunny for extended periods, although continued snow cover in the mountains means that most walking paths are still not yet open. Summer can be frustratingly variable – when the sun comes out, it can get very hot, sometimes too hot, but it is often grey and rainy with a regular occurrence of thunderstorms both over the lakes and mountains. Lugano, in particular, is noted for its summer thunderstorms. However, some of the best weather is in late summer and early autumn, when many people come to walk. The weather then changes for the worse in November and the first snows begin to fall in December. The winter season often lasts till Easter.

The forecasts given in local Ticino newspapers are usually reliable (and easy to understand for non-Italian speakers); mountain huts also give walkers detailed weather forecasts.

Above: 'Rabadan' – carnival in Bellinzona

Below: Isole di Brissago, Lake Maggiore

DRIVING IN SWITZERLAND

Swiss roads are well maintained and very safe. With spectacular engineering works in the form of bridges and tunnels, routes through the treacherous terrain of the Alps are usually very fast. The centre of Lugano can get clogged up with traffic at busy times, but other than that roads are generally uncongested. As regards routes, the main valleys have two or more routes running parallel through them – one for motorway traffic, the other a more minor road: this is the case with the Bellinzona-Airolo roads up to the Gotthard tunnel, and also the Bellinzona-San Bernardino route to the San Bernardino tunnel. These two tunnels are operational all year; the San Bernardino and San Gottardo road passes, which go the 'scenic way' over the top of the pass, avoiding the tunnels, are not cleared of snow and so are closed between around November and April. The Nufenenpass/Passo della Novena (Chapter One) and the Passo del Lucomagno/Lukmanier Pass (Chapter Two) are also closed in winter, with no tunnel alternatives.

Motorways

The Swiss love their motorways! The network links the northern centres (Zurich, Lucerne and Basel) with other parts of Switzerland, Germany, France, and Italy. Some motorways are classified 'semi-motorways' – they are marked on signs by a white car on a green background, rather than the white carriageways on a green background, which indicates a full motorway. To drive on the latter it is necessary to pay a yearly tax; it is also necessary to have paid this tax to use the Gotthard and San Bernardino road tunnels *(see page 134)*.

Motorways are given two numbers: the 'N' number is for the national network, and the 'E' number refers to the pan-European motorway network. The main motorway running through the Ticino, on the Milan-Como-Chiasso-Lugano-Bellinzona-Airolo-Gotthard tunnel route, is the N2/E35. Beyond the Gotthard there are motorway links to Lucerne, Zurich and Basel, and on into Germany and France. The Bellinzona-Chur motorway (which runs through the San Bernardino tunnel) is the N13. Beyond Chur the motorway runs up to St Gallen and Lake Constance, giving a route into Austria and Germany.

Rules and regulations

- Car drivers should be aged 18 or over.
- Ascending vehicles on mountain passes have right of way, unless it's a postbus in which case it has right of way whichever direction it's going.
- Traffic on roundabouts has priority.
- Seatbelts should always be worn if they are fitted.
- A red warning triangle should always be carried (preferably not in the boot).

- Penalties for drinking and driving are high, and the limit (0.8 per cent) is comparatively low.
- Drive on the right, and always give way to traffic coming from the right.
- Headlights should always be used in tunnels.
- Speed limits are 50kph in towns, 80kph on normal roads, and 100 or 120kph on motorways depending on their exact status as 'semi' or 'full' motorways. For those towing a caravan the limit is always 80kph.
- The road sign showing a yellow bugle on a square background indicates that drivers must heed the instructions of post bus drivers.

Breakdown

The Touring Club der Schweiz (TCS) runs the country's breakdown service (☎ 140). It's free of use to those who are members of its affiliated national motoring organisations, such as the AA or RAC (though check your membership terms before you leave to ensure that their services are included in your membership arrangements).

Car rental

Although fairly straightforward, it is best to arrange before leaving as on-the-spot rental is considerably more expensive than pre-arranged booking with companies such as Avis and Hertz. If renting locally ask the tourist office for addresses of local car-rental firms; you'll find that Swiss or Ticinese firms charge lower rates than the international companies. However, international firms may be more willing to provide paperwork in English – it's unwise to sign up for car rental if you don't fully understand the Italian small print. The following numbers are UK central reservation numbers:

Hertz
☎ (0990) 996699
Rental garages and offices in Lugano, Locarno and Zurich Airport.

Avis
☎ (0870) 606 0100
Rental garage and offices in Lugano and Zurich Airport.

Budget
☎ (0800) 181181
Rental garage at Zurich Airport. No Ticino office.

Europcar
☎ (0345) 222525
Rental garages and offices at Zurich Airport and Lugano.

Holiday autos
☎ (0870) 530 0400
Rental garage and office at Zurich Airport. No Ticino office.

ELECTRICITY

The electric current is 220V, 50Hz. Appliances which work on 240V will operate satisfactorily in Switzerland, but for other pieces of electrical equipment a transformer is needed. North American appliances, which are made to work at 60Hz, may be under-powered when operated by the Swiss mains. All electrical equipment brought from the UK will have to be plugged into the mains by a continental adapter, which allows British square-pin plugs to be plugged into the round-pin sockets in Switzerland. There is usually no problem in finding spare power points in hotel rooms from which electrical equipment can be operated.

EMERGENCIES

Police	☎ 117
Fire brigade	☎ 118
Ambulance	☎ 144
Road breakdown assistance	☎ 140

ENTRY AND CUSTOMS REGULATIONS AND DIPLOMATIC REPRESENTATION

Citizens of English-speaking countries do not need visas to visit Switzerland; maximum stay is three months but passports are rarely stamped (although they are usually inspected, at both airports and land crossings). In theory Swiss citizens are required to carry a form of personal identification at all times, and so, therefore, are visitors. It is wise to keep a photocopy of the most important pages in your passport, and a record of the passport number, as a precaution against loss or theft.

Swiss Embassies Overseas

UK
16-18 Montague Place,
London W1H 2BQ
☎ (020) 7616 6000

USA
Cathedral Avenue NW,
Washington, DC 20008-3499
☎ (202) 745 7900

CANADA
5 Marlborough Avenue,
Ottawa, Ontario KIN 8E6
☎ (613) 235 1837

Consulates – Zurich

UK
Dufourstrasse 56 ☎ (01) 383 6560

USA
Zollikerstrasse 141 ☎ (01) 422 2566

CANADA maintains an embassy in Bern, at Kirchenfeldstrasse 88
☎ (01) 357 3200

Consulates –Milan

UK
Via San Paolo 7 ☎ (02) 723 001

USA
Via Amedeo 2/10 ☎ (02) 659 6561

CANADA
Via Pisani 19 ☎ (02) 675 81

All personal requirements for a trip to Switzerland can be taken into the country free of charge, including film, video and camping equipment, and gifts to the value of SF100. Those over 17 can take in 2 litres of alcoholic beverages (up to 15 per cent) and 1 litres of beverages over 15 per cent; plus 200 cigarettes, 50 cigars and 9oz of tobacco. These latter allowances are doubled for visitors from outside Europe.

FESTIVALS, EVENTS AND HOLIDAYS

Shrove Tuesday: Risotto eating in the Piazzas of Ascona, Losone and Arcegno; carnival in Bellinzona with risotto eating in the open air.

Maundy Thursday: Medieval procession at Mendrisio.

March-July: Spring concerts, Lugano.

June: New Orleans Festival in Ascona.

June-July: Jazz Festival in Lugano.

August 1st: Swiss National Day. Fireworks in the evening over Lake Lugano.

August: Locarno International Film Festival (first two weeks).

August-October: Ascona International Music Festival; concerts on the Island of Brissago.

October: Vine Growers Festival Procession (first Sunday in month), Lugano.

Public holidays

(Those marked * are specific to Canton Ticino and are not followed by the whole country):

January 1 (New Year)

January 6 (Epiphany*)

March 19 S. Giuseppe (St Joseph)

Easter Sunday and Monday

40th Day after Easter: Ascension Day

7th week after Easter: Whit Sunday and Monday

May 1 (Labour Day*)

2nd Thursday after Whitsun (Corpus Christi*)

June 29 (St Peter and St Paul)

August 1 (Swiss National Day)

August 15 Ascension of the Virgin Mary

Third Sunday in September (Federal Thanksgiving Day)

November 1 (All Saints Day*)

December 8 Immaculate Conception

25 December

26 December (St Stephen's Day)

The above days count as 'Sundays' as far as opening times and timetables are concerned.

HEALTH CARE

There is no state health care system in Switzerland so if you need any sort of medical attention you will have to pay for it. For this reason it is highly advisable to take out a comprehensive health insurance policy before you leave. Initial costs of health care will have to be paid out in Switzerland and will be refunded later by the insurers. Check when taking out policies that it includes outdoor activities that you may wish to take part in – mountaineering, skiing, white-water rafting etc. If you need medical care, ask a pharmacist, hotel or tourist office to recommend a doctor *(medico)* who speaks English. In an emergency head for a hospital *(ospedale)* and casualty *(ponto soccorso)*, or dial 144 for an *ambulanza.*

Pharmacies *(farmacia)* are easy to identify by the green cross outside their doors. Not surprisingly, they are well stocked, but not many products have information in English and brand names are often different in Switzerland than back home. Keep all medications brought from home in their original container, and learn the generic rather than the brand name for drugs, which will make obtaining repeat prescriptions easier.

Food and water are unlikely to pose any problems as regards health. Tap water is safe to drink, as is water from drinking fountains in villages and by farms, which many hikers use (though look out for the sign *acqua non potabile*, which means it isn't drinkable). However, water out of streams isn't safe and should be purified by boiling thoroughly (for five minutes) or by the addition of iodine tablets, sold in pharmacies.

The most obvious hazards are those associated with the mountains. You can become sunburned very easily in the thin air, so wear a hat, sunglasses and sun-cream. Likewise, it can get cold in the mountains very suddenly, and to prevent hypothermia *always* carry extra layers of clothing and also waterproofs – being caught outside without adequate clothing in cold, wet, windy weather is a sure-fire route to problems from bodily heat loss. Dehydration and lack of food do not help matters, so walkers should always have plenty of liquids and sugar-rich food such as chocolate with them. Altitude sickness is unlikely to be a problem as it only kicks in around 11,483ft (3,500m) and upwards – higher than most mountains in the Ticino.

Those prone to motion sickness might want to bring some preventative medication out with them, particularly to combat the nausea-inducing corkscrew twists which some roads make as they climb steeply up mountainsides.

Ticks can be a nuisance, particularly if you are camping near rivers or forests, so insect cream and repellent might be a good idea. Rabies is present in Switzerland, as it is in all of continental Europe, and assistance should always be sought for those who have been bitten by animals (including dogs, foxes, cats and bats). A number of snakes are native to the region, although it is very rare to see them, and even rarer to be bitten by one. Again, a snake bite needs medical attention (although it will not be fatal), and beware of putting your hand in holes or crevices in rocks where snakes might be lurking.

It is worth bearing in mind that health care is much cheaper in neighbouring Italy, where UK citizens can receive free health care and reduced price medication with an E111 form (obtainable from post offices in the UK). This form is completely useless in Switzerland as it is for European Union countries and citizens only.

MAPS

Switzerland must be one of the most efficiently and thoroughly mapped countries in the world. The central mapping authority is the Bundesamt fur Landestopographie (BL or OFT in French) which covers the whole of Switzerland in three map series, 1:100,000, 1:50,000 and, the most detailed, 1:25,000. There's a huge amount of detail, and maps are very accurately drawn and regularly updated; the 1:25,000 maps are excellent for walkers, and twenty-two of them cover the area covered by this book. The 1:50,000 maps are also good for walkers, and cover the Ticino in seven maps. There are also two specific 1:50,000 tourist-oriented maps which cover parts of the Ticino – one for the Gotthard region, and one for the Locarno/Lugano region. A number of maps are available which cover the whole of the Ticino canton. You will also find specialist walking maps available, produced by the Swiss Hikers' Federation and other organisations, printed on more weather-resistant paper – these are the best maps for finding different mountain routes, identifying postbus stops, and mountain shelters and huts.

The only drawback is that these maps are fairly expensive, so decide carefully which ones you will need to use for the areas you will be covering. Bear in mind that the immense amount of detail in the 1:25,000 maps can be a drawback as well as an advantage, as these maps cover a limited amount of geographical area. Map sellers do not mind prospective customers folding out maps and looking at them carefully before deciding which ones to buy. Some maps are not printed with a key *(legende)*, but this is available on a separate sheet from most outlets; these include tourist offices, book stalls, railways stations and hotels.

MEDIA

English-language internationally-published newspapers such as the American *International Herald Tribune* (published in Zurich), the *USA today*, and European editions of British newspapers (in particular the *Guardian*), are available promptly at station news kiosks in Bellinzona, Lugano and Locarno, but are difficult to find beyond these outlets. British newspapers such as the *Daily Telegraph* and *The Times* can also usually be bought, one or two days after their UK day of publication, at these outlets.

A short wave radio will give the best access to international radio services in English such as the BBC World Service, Voice of America, and the English-language broadcasts of Swiss Radio International. Frequencies change throughout the day. The BBC gives frequency information on its information line in the UK ☎ (08700) 100222; in Switzerland its broadcasts can be picked up on short wave only on 9410, 6195 and 12095 kHz. Reception is poor around Airolo but fine in most other places. Ironically it is sometimes possible to pick up BBC Radio 4 in Airolo, in just about listenable quality.

Hotels with three or more stars usually have a TV in the room, where a variety of Swiss and Italian TV stations can be watched. Channel One of the Swiss Broadcasting Service often broadcasts in English. Other stations usually broadcast dubbed foreign programmes and films. In the more expensive hotels, TVs will be able to receive English-language satellite services such as CNN, MTV and Eurosport, in addition to rather more dubious fare offered by Italian satellite networks.

POST AND TELEPHONE SERVICES

Postal services are run by the Swiss Postal Service, *La Posta* to Italian speakers. Post Offices are generally open from Monday to Friday 8am-noon and 2-6pm, and on Saturday mornings 8-11am. Smaller branches may only be open for limited hours, with a longer lunch break. In some really remote areas, postal services are provided by mobile post vans, which park up for a few hours each day or week. There are two post rates: 'A' (priority) rate means letters will be delivered the next day in Switzerland, and 3-5 days for international destinations; 'B'-rates (Economy) are slower.

To receive mail, ask the sender to write the address in this way: John SMITH, Poste Restante, Posta, Lugano-1, 6901 Lugano, Switzerland; writing a '1' means that post will be sent to the main post office in the town. The other postal codes are:

Ascona	6612
Bellinzona	6500
Biasca	6710
Airolo	6780
Locarno	6601
Mendrisio	6850

Telephone services are operated by Swisscom. Public phone boxes are plentiful and invariably work well; you can opt for instructions in English. Payment is by phone cards (available from hotels and post offices) or by credit cards (most UK credit cards issued by Visa and other internationally recognised groups will work). The code to dial out of the country is 00, followed by 44 for the UK and 1 for North America. Virtually all phone boxes have a key pad, and small computer screen from which e-mail messages can be sent.

The cheap rate to Europe is 9pm to 8am weekdays and all day at weekends, to North America it's 11pm to 10am and throughout the weekend. Telegrams, telexes and faxes can be sent from post offices (try to find a self-service machine – getting counter staff to do it costs more).

Useful numbers

111 Internal directory enquiries.

191 International directory enquiries (192 for Germany; 193 for France).

091 Area code for the Ticino (omit the 0 when calling from overseas).

0041 International code for Switzerland from UK.

OUTDOOR ACTIVITIES

Skiing

Switzerland is of course a skier's paradise, but the big ski resorts are all elsewhere in the country, in French and German speaking areas. The Ticino mountains are not high enough, and the snow melts too early and falls too late for skiing of the standard in other parts of Switzerland. The biggest resort is Airolo (Chapter One), where there are four cableways and 11 miles (18km) of cross-country ski tracks. Other popular areas are San Bernardino (Chapter Three); Leontica (Chapter Two); Bosco Gurin (Chapter Five); Cardada (above Locarno, Chapter Four); Monte Lema, just above Lugano, and Monte Tamaro, only 15 minutes along the motorway and very popular with the locals (Chapter Six); and Carì, above Faido (Chapter One), very sunny and ideal for families with children.

Cycling

Bicycles can be hired at railway stations; ask there or at tourist offices for more details. Those on offer include mountain bikes, tandems and cycles for children. Bicycles can normally be handed back at any station, unless you borrow them for only half a day, in which case they must be given back to the same station. Bikes can be transported on most trains (not Intercity) for a small fee, which normally allows several journeys to be made during any one day. The Swiss Bike Pass, available from stations, allows free transport for bikes on buses, trains and boats, and free bike rental.

Fishing

Local tourist offices can supply a fishing permit which covers the whole canton. Fishing is allowed year-round on Lakes Maggiore and Lugano, and from April to September in other lakes and rivers. Swiss Tourist Offices have a brochure about angling opportunities.

Golf and tennis

A number of top-class hotels have tennis courts; if you fancy a game, try asking them whether they will let non-residents play. Tourist offices

The lake front at Locarno

have brochures on specific tennis holidays, which may give more information. Two golf courts in the region are:
Patriziale Ascona Golf Club, Via al Lido 81, Ascona (18 holes) and **Lugano Golf Club**, Magliaso (18 holes).

Water sports

Enquire at local tourist offices for details about canoeing in the Ticino and Verzasca rivers, and the sailing and windsurfing schools and facilities on the lakes.

TOURIST INFORMATION

In Ticino

Switzerland more or less invented the concept of organised tourism and its tourist infrastructure is arguably the most efficient in the world. There are fifteen tourist offices spread throughout the Ticino (for addresses see the end of each chapter), all of them with English-speaking staff who are knowledgeable about the local area and willing to be of assistance.

A lot of tourist information brochures and leaflets are available, usually published in four languages (German, French, Italian and English). Although some of the leaflets are on the glossy side, it doesn't take that much browsing or asking to find hard practical information. Tourist offices are usually happy to help travellers find accommodation and will ring round hotels free of charge in their particular locality.

Offices are known in Italian as *ufficio turistico* and can be identified by the internationally recognised '*i*' symbol; they are usually open during office hours (with an hour or two break for lunch) and on Saturday mornings. In addition, computer terminals carrying tourist information are located in railway stations, tourist offices etc; they carry databases on hotels, sporting facilities etc.

The tourist office for the whole of Canton Ticino is in Bellinzona:

Ticino Turismo
Via Lugano 12
CH-6500 Bellinzona
☎ (091) 825 7056
Fax (091) 825 3614
e-mail: ett@www.tourism-ticino.ch

The regional tourist board for the Ticino maintains a website, with information in English, although its sections on climate, culture etc are fairly thin compared to what is in this book. The site is best used for the monthly cultural events listings, although there is also a webcam and a number of photos: http://www.tourism-ticino.ch/

Outside Ticino

Tourist information offices outside Switzerland are very efficient and can supply plenty of information relating to accommodation, festivals, package holidays, travel arrangements etc. Addresses include:

UK
Switzerland Tourism
Swiss Centre
Swiss Court (off Leicester Square)
London W1V 8EE
☎ (020) 7734 1921
Fax (020) 7437 4577
e-mail: stc@stlondon.com

USA
Switzerland Tourism
Swiss Centre
608 Fifth Avenue
New York NY 10020
☎ (212) 757 5944
Fax (212) 262 6116
e-mail:
info.usa@switzerlandtourism.ch

CANADA
Switzerland Tourism
Contact numbers:
☎ (416) 695 2090
Fax (416) 695 2774
e-mail:
infocaen@switzerlandtourism.ch

The main national tourist office
websites are better than the Ticino
one, with information about public
transport, package holidays and
other practical aspects of visiting
the country. There's also a good
collection of photos.
UK: http://
www.switzerlandtourism.ch/

USA: http://
www.myswitzerland.com/

PUBLIC TRANSPORT

Switzerland has one of the best integrated and most extensive public
transport systems in the world. Within the Ticino a network of trains,
buses, boats (on Lakes Lugano and Maggiore) and cable cars can take
those without vehicles more or less anywhere they want to go. Bus
and train timetables are often integrated, so that the arrival of a bus or
train allows for connections to be made with departing buses or trains
(bus and rail stations are usually next door to one another).

Services throughout the country are usually frequent, and information is easy to obtain – bus and rail timetables are freely available at rail
stations, tourist offices and in hotels. A combined timetable for all bus,
train and cable car services in the Ticino can be bought from rail stations and tourist offices. The only drawback with public transport is
that it is not particularly cheap, but costs can be reduced by the use of
one of a number of passes.

Information about the available travel passes is available at rail
stations and tourist offices. Within the Ticino, there's a pass for
unlimited boat, train and bus travel around the Locarno/Maggiore
region for a week, with additional benefits for travel around Lugano. A
cheaper version of the same pass gives free travel for only three days
and reductions for another four days. Another pass serves the Lugano
region and includes journeys up the two funiculars, with reductions for
travel in the Locarno area. These passes are usually only available
between March and October.

Passes covering the whole country, best purchased from tourist
offices outside Switzerland include:

Swisspass	Unlimited travel on boats, trains, Alpine postbuses, reductions on private railways; available for 4, 8, 15 days or 1 month.
Swiss Flexipass	As above, but for any 3 days in a 15 day period.
Half-fare travel card	Intended for motorists. An unlimited number of bus and train tickets can be purchased at 50 per cent of the normal price. Usually valid for one month.
Family card	Allows children aged six to sixteen to travel free of charge on trains and buses if accompanied by one adult. Free if you purchase one of the above passes from Swiss Travel Centres. Can be purchased in Switzerland, in which case there is an additional benefit for sixteen to twenty-five year olds, they can travel at half the usual fare if travelling with at least one parent.
Ticino card	Allows the owner to ski anywhere in the Ticino (and selected places in the nearby Cantons if there is little snow locally) from Monday to Friday. It also gives free access to all mountain lifts, rack railways, cable cars in the Ticino and all boats on the lakes.

Information about these and other passes is available on:

http://www.switzerlandtourism.ch/uk/uk_traveld.html

Rail services

The rail service is run by Swiss Federal Railways (in Italian, FFS: Ferrovia Federale Svizzera). Trains are reliable, fast, comfortable and punctual. The main route through the Ticino emerges from the Gotthard tunnel at Airolo, then runs through Biasca, Bellinzona, Lugano and then Chiasso. At Bellinzona there is a branch line to Locarno. Chiasso is on the border with Italy and some trains head on from here to Como, and then Milan. Trains passing through the Gotthard run to and from major centres in northern Switzerland (Lucerne, Zurich, Basel and Schaffhausen) and further afield into Germany.

There are two private rail lines in the Ticino: the Centovalli rail line from Locarno to Domodossola in Italy, and the Monte Generoso rack railway which runs from Capolago to the summit of Monte Generoso above Lake Lugano. If you buy a pass, check whether it includes free or reduced travel on these lines, and on the many cable cars in the region.

Some of the services operating on the main line are ultra-swish, private Italian *Cisalpino* services which tilt to travel round corners quickly and serve only major centres. These trains operate on the Milan-Como-Lugano-Bellinzona-Gotthard route to Zurich, Basel and

Germany (and also pass through Domodossola, at the end of the Centovalli line from Locarno, which is on the Milan-Brig-Geneva route). A supplement is required on these trains for travel in Italy, or into Italy, but not for internal journeys within Switzerland (but double check this at stations before boarding). Some Cisalpino trains require advance seat reservation too (look out for the letter 'R' in a box on timetables).

Other, slower, trains carry various labels (including Intercity, Eurocity, and slower, *regionale* services) according to how fast they travel and how many stops they make. Always make sure the train you get on actually stops at the station you want to get off at, and doesn't whizz past it in a blur of speed!

Tickets are expensive and a pass is likely to save you money if you are going to do any amount of travelling by train. There are rarely queues at booking offices, and main stations including Bellinzona, Lugano and Locarno have automatic machines from which you can buy tickets using most foreign credit cards (you will need to use your PIN number). Some of the smallest stations have no booking office, and tickets must be bought from machines before boarding trains.

Free timetables, each covering a specific route, are easily available . There is a full Swiss rail timetable available on http://www.sbb.ch, and most train times in the Ticino and Switzerland are in the Thomas Cook European Rail Timetable, published every month and available from Thomas Cook offices or booksellers.

First class tickets cost 65 per cent more than second class tickets. Return trips are cheaper only for longer journeys. Most stations have left luggage facilities and will allow you to send your luggage on to your next destination to be picked up later.

Trains are often the best place from which to appreciate the magnificent scenery of the Ticino. The most scenic sections of line are: Capolago to Monte Generoso (cog railway, page 121), Locarno to Domodossola (Centovalli Line, page 80); on the main line the most scenic stretches are between Mendrisio and Lugano (along the shores of the lake) and Biasca to Airolo, where the line ascends the side of the valley in a series of spirals at one point to gain height.

Buses

Most buses are run by the postal services and so are known as post buses *(autopostale).* In rural areas the bus driver is responsible for collecting and delivering mail sacks from and to the tiny village post offices along the route. For these reasons, virtually every settlement in Switzerland is covered by a bus service at least once a day.

Bus stops are usually next to post offices, and they also stop outside railway stations, ensuring an integrated road and rail transport system. In a few places (such as Bellinzona to Locarno, and Airolo to Bellinzona) bus routes follow rail routes (buses are invariably slower); in many places there is no duplication of routes, however.

In a couple of places private bus firms operate bus services instead of the post office. These include the Val Blenio, where bus services from Biasca to Olivone, the Passo del Lucomagno and other places covered in Chapter Two, are operated by Autolinee Bleniesi. Also, the Centovalli and Val Maggia (as far as Bignasco), along which services from Locarno operate, are run by Ferrovie Autolinee Regionali Ticinesi (FART).

Timetables are easy to come by – pick up the yellow booklets from buses themselves, tourist offices, hotels or railway stations. Ticino is divided into five timetabling regions: Airolo and the Leventina Valley (Chapter One); Bellinzona, Biasca, and routes leading to Olivone and the Passo del San Bernardino (Chapters Two and Three); Locarno and the valleys (Chapters Four and Five); Lugano and the northern edge of Lake Lugano (Chapter Six); and Mendrisio/Chiasso (also Chapter Six). The timetables are quite easy to understand; the word *feriale* means 'workdays', which usually includes Saturdays. Unless otherwise stated, services are reduced on Sundays and holidays.

Those contemplating a lot of bus travel should buy one of the passes described at the beginning of this section. Tickets are usually purchased from the driver when boarding (note that in Italy a different system is in operation and tickets usually have to be purchased from ticket offices before boarding).

Long distance bus travel is not common in Switzerland. One exception is the Lugano-St Moritz bus service, which passes through Italy linking the lakeside resort with one of the premier ski resorts in eastern Switzerland. In this case tickets usually have to be purchased in advance. Unaccompanied luggage can be transported by buses for a fee, and picked up at post offices – a useful service for hikers.

Internal flights

Switzerland's small size and excellent surface transport means that the expensive and fairly limited internal air services are unlikely to be used by many visitors. From Lugano Airport at Agno, west of the city (and linked to Lugano station by a shuttlebus), Crossair operates flights to Basel, Bern, Zurich and Geneva. There are no internal services within Ticino itself.

City transport

The city bus networks in Locarno, Lugano and Bellinzona are based on automatic ticket machines at bus stops, which display routes carefully, but drivers will usually sell tickets too. Tickets sometimes specify a time limit, ie you can keep using the ticket until the time printed on it is exceeded, however, this will probably apply to a single bus route. Day passes are available (contact railway stations or ticket offices). Inspectors on buses carry out regular checks and can fine people on the spot for having no ticket. Taxis are expensive, and congregate outside railway stations.

Lakes and mountains

Travelling by boat or aerial cableway is half the fun of visiting the lakes and mountains. There are passenger boat services on Lakes Maggiore, Como and Lugano all year round, although services are reduced in winter. National travel passes can be used on some of these services. Slick, fast hydrofoil services operate on Lake Maggiore . There's also a car ferry on the Italian part of Maggiore, linking Laveno (Chapter Four) with Verbania on the opposite shore.

In the mountains, there is a variety of forms of railway and cableway to get you up to the views. If you have a transport pass check whether it allows for discounts, or even free travel, on the following services. The cable cars *(funivia)* at Robiei and Airolo are one-cabin cars slung under wires capable of transporting up to 100 people at a time. Other cable cars, such as Monte Lema, Monte Tamaro and Serpiano, only sit about four people and are clamped onto the moving cable at the start of the journey, a process which involves various clanking sounds and wobbles, before the car rushes up into the air. Chairlifts *(seggovia)*, such as those at Leontica and Bosco Gurin are chairs suspended by a cable, open to the weather.

All aerial cable ways may close for periods of reconstruction which may be anything up to a year, so check at tourist offices first if your plans depend on them being operational. Some cable ways are only operational in winter for skiers, others only in summer for walkers, but most operate year-round.

As regards rail transport in the mountains, the funicular railway *(funicolare)* at Piotta, operated by the national rail network, is the steepest in the world. Two cars, both running on rails, are hauled (or restrained) by cables, and counter-balance one another, passing at the half-way point. There's another funicular in Lugano, linking the railway station with the town centre, and two more just outside the town (Paradiso to Monte San Salvatore and Castagnola to Monte Brè). The region's only rack railway, where cogs under the train engage with a specially toothed rail to assist ascent and breaking, runs from Capolago on Lake Lugano to Monte Generoso (see page 121).

LANDMARK VISITORS

(See page 159 for mailing details)

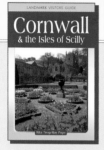

Cornwall*
ISBN: 1 901522 09 1
256pp, £10.95

Devon
ISBN: 1 901522 42 3
224pp, £9.95

Dorset
ISBN: 1 901522 46 6
240pp, £9.95

Somerset
ISBN: 1 901522 40 7
224pp, £10.95

Cotswolds
ISBN: 1 901522 12 1
224pp, £9.99

Hampshire
ISBN: 1 901522 14 8
224pp, £9.95

East Anglia
ISBN: 1 901522 58 X
224pp, £9.95

Scotland*
ISBN: 1 901522 18 0
288pp, £11.95

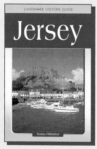

Jersey
ISBN: 1 901522 47 4
224pp, £9.99

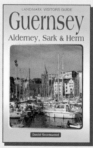

Guernsey
ISBN: 1 901522 48 2
224pp, £9.95

Harrogate
ISBN: 1 901522 55 5
96pp, £4.95

GUIDES TO THE UK

Lake District*
ISBN: 1 901522 38 5
224pp, £9.95

Peak District
ISBN: 1 901522 25 3
240pp, £9.99

Yorkshire Dales
ISBN: 1 901522 41 5
224pp, £10.95

West Cornwall
ISBN: 1 901522 24 5
96pp, £5.95

South Devon
ISBN: 1 901522 52 0
96pp, £5.95

Southern Peak
ISBN: 1 901522 27 X
96pp, £5.95

Southern Lakeland
ISBN: 1 901522 53 9
96pp, £5.95

Dartmoor
ISBN: 1 901522 69 5
96pp, £5.95

New Forest
ISBN: 1 901522 70 9
96pp, £5.95

Isle of Wight
ISBN: 1 901522 71 7
96pp, £5.95

Hereford
ISBN: 1 901522 72 5
96pp, £5.95

Prices subject to alteration from time to time

LANDMARK
VISITORS GUIDES

US & British VI*
ISBN: 1 901522 03 2
256pp, £11.95

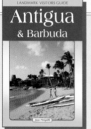

Antigua & Barbuda*
ISBN: 1 901522 02 4
96pp, £5.95

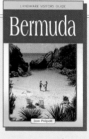

Bermuda*
ISBN: 1 901522 07 5
160pp, £7.95

Dominican Republic*
ISBN: 1 90152208 3
160pp, £7.95

New Zealand*
ISBN: 1 901522 36 9
320pp, £12.95

Northern Cyprus
ISBN: 1 901522 51 2
176pp, £9.95

Orlando*
ISBN: 1 901522 22 9
256pp, £9.95

Florida: Gulf Coast*
ISBN: 1 901522 01 6
160pp, £7.95

Florida: The Keys*
ISBN: 1 901522 21 0
160pp, £7.95

St Lucia*
ISBN: 1 901522 28 8
144pp, £6.95

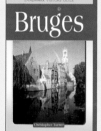

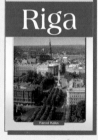

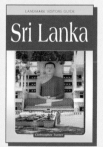

Published by
Landmark Publishing Ltd,
Waterloo House, 12 Compton, Ashbourne, Derbyshire DE6 1DA England
Tel: (01335) 347349 Fax: (01335) 347303 e-mail: landmark@clara.net

ISBN 1 901 522 74 1

British Library Cataloguing in Publication Data: a catalogue record for this
book is available from the British Library.

Print: Gutenberg Press Ltd, Malta
Cartography: James Allsopp & Samantha Witham
Design: Samantha Witham

Front cover: Ascona, on Lake Maggiore
Back cover top: Around Robiei; **bottom:** Lago Ritòm

Picture Credits:
Andrew Beattie: Front & back cover (both), 3, 6,10, 15TR, 18, 27 all, 30, 31
both, 38, 39, 42TL, 42B, 47, 58 both, 59 both, 63, 67B, 70, 71B, 74BL, 78, 82,
83B, 86, 91T, 95T, 103B, 111 all, 114, 147
Tim Pepper: 75, 106B, 123, 126, 127
Ticino Turismo: 11 both, 15TL, 15B, 22, 23, 26 both, 34, 42TR, 46, 50, 55, 62,
66 both, 67T, 71T, 74T, 74BR, 79, 83T, 90, 91B, 94, 98, 103T, 106T, 110 both,
118, 119 both, 131, 138B
Juliusz Komarnicki: 95B, 115, 138T